DEATH AND THE CITY

DEATH AND THE CITY

On Loss, Mourning, and Melancholia at Work

Susan Kahn

First published in 2017 by
Karnac Books Ltd
118 Finchley Road, London NW3 5HT

British Library Cataloguing in Publication Data

A C.I.P. for this book is available from the British Library

ISBN 978 1 78220 354 4

Edited, designed and produced by The Studio Publishing Services Ltd
www.publishingservicesuk.co.uk
e-mail: studio@publishingservicesuk.co.uk

Printed in Great Britain by TJ International Ltd, Padstow, Cornwall

www.karnacbooks.com

CONTENTS

DEATH AT WORK

ACKNOWLEDGEMENTS

My thanks go to the staff at Interbank, who shared so much in interviews and allowed me to observe their demise. Their contribution as the subjects of my gaze is greatly appreciated and acknowledged. Special thanks must go to my research angel, Anna, who opened the doors to the organisation and then allowed me to stay for such a very long time.

I am very grateful to Dr Andreas Liefooghe, my supervisor, my mentor, and my companion on the Royal Road. We have been through a life cycle together and I hope we share many more beginnings and endings. I would also like to acknowledge the insights of Professor Josh Cohen, Dr Rael Meyerowitz, Professor Emma Bell, Ross Lazar, Dr Sheila White, and Dr Keith Barrett, all of whom have increased my understanding, given me support, and shared their knowledge. A particular thank you to Professor Lionel Stapley, who introduced my work to the Karnac team, who have been a pleasure to work with. The two organisations that have provided a constant stream of enormously rich learning and creativity are OPUS and ISPSO; my membership of these bodies and the community of inspiring and challenging thinkers has greatly enriched me.

The love and support of my sublime home team, Neville, Victoria, Charlie, and Sam, has been a constant blessing—thank you.

ABOUT THE AUTHOR

Susan Kahn was first an anthropologist and now works as a consultant, coach, and mediator. Her expertise is in the complexities of working life with a particular specialism in conflict at work, group dynamics, and the underlying mechanisms of leadership and teamwork. She is also a faculty member in the Organizational Psychology Department at Birkbeck, University of London, and works as a group relations consultant with Opus. Her doctoral research focused on endings in organisations and the experience of working through crisis, change, and closure. Part of a large family, she is married with three children.

For Norma and Baruj Levy
who taught me how to live, and how to die

FOREWORD

This is an elegantly positioned book. It simultaneously welcomes the psychoanalytic practitioner, the organisational consultant, the executive coach, and the ordinary leader. It conveys depth, knowledge, and humanity. *Death and the City* feels internationally relevant, offering insight into how to make sense of our increasingly complex and interconnected working world, a world of existential crisis, be that economic collapse, natural disaster, industrial accident, or an ethical failure, that can cause the closure of a department, the end of a CEO's career, or the death of the whole organisation. Equally, internal crises—individual behaviours, reckless self-serving decision making, incentivising workers for the short term over the long term—can also cause dramatic, unexpected endings. Personal and systemic stress and distress is an almost invariable and inevitable outcome.

This book invites us to think about organisational behaviours, which, of course, are anchored in the actions and psychology of the people who work in them. So, be it the junior newcomer, the experienced personal assistant, or a highly paid and powerful senior leader, every employee has the potential to shape their organisation and its outcomes. From hope and optimism to resistance and cynicism, each kind of response can contribute to a living, a thriving, a toxic, or a dying organisation.

How many of us have been part of mourning conversations after redundancies are announced, when a cover-up is revealed, following the sudden departure of a top-flight executive, or when an employee commits suicide?

Arguably, seemingly negative cycles or "deaths" can produce phoenix-like inspiration, resilience, and re-emergence, like the cleansing and fresh shoots which sprout after a devastating forest fire. Failure can produce creativity as a response. It might create something better than what went before. This book has the potential to help leaders become conscious of when they are feeding such cycles of destruction and renewal. Complete avoidance of endings or death might not always be healthy, but conscious leadership and conscious attempts by leaders to understand what went wrong, or could start to go wrong, could have the potential to avert calamity in the first place. Leaders might, instead, choose to invest their energy in taking their organisation forward with enlightenment and wisdom, rather than expending their resources in mutually destructive rivalry, panicky but futile salvage attempts, or slumped slow death followed by mourning and regret.

Leaders might be more willing to examine strategic mistakes, dressed up in apparently sophisticated management-speak, than to explore their more primitive thinking and behaviours. Failing to understand how people and systems react to crisis, drama, or threat of extinction risks missing a vital seam of rich learning and understanding. Exploring fear and death and how our survival instincts can either avert the worst, or cause it to come sooner, might help organisations become more robust and sustainable.

Death and the City anchors the observed behaviours of employees in a collapsing bank in psychological and psychoanalytic theory. However, it does so in an integrated way, so that we do not miss a moment of the narrative. It exposes how workers at every level of an organisation become increasingly self-centred and desperate to protect their interests, their income, their family's standard of living, their professional reputation, and their sense of self-esteem, or even the health of their marriage. The book moves, through psychoanalytic and organisational studies' theory, to tackle mourning, melancholia, the death drive, and defences at work.

Small, nimble start-ups to large, established organisations assume their permanence—yet repeating death cycles seems obvious and almost inevitable. This book offers the possibility of an alternative: a bridge from psychoanalytic thought to the concerns and experiences of the business world and back again. A mutually nourishing experience, that every employee could benefit from. A new way for leaders to lead their people with the potential for a new format of how we run our companies, and what we expect authentic leadership to be like. It could change how we face endings, closure, merger, or acquisition at work.

With greater willingness to explore early an organisation's unravelling, there is the hope of rescue and sustainability, the potential to adapt and be flexible, for leaders to harness the behavioural data in front of them, and inside them, in order to avert death, or, if the death of an organisation is necessary, to co-create a healthy ending.

This book might be about the slow death of one organisation, but it offers a template through which to analyse many other individuals and systems and encourages us not to assume that the big names are immortal and will endure forever. It asks us to consider every organisation as potentially fragile.

Every leader should read this book; every business school and MBA programme should engage with its themes.

Rachel Ellison, MBE

Rachel Ellison is an executive leadership coach with expert knowledge of challenging, changing, multicultural environments. She coaches CEOs, board level and high potential talent in the City and globally.

Introduction

Organisational death deserves contemplation at a time when organisations are experiencing more exposure to endings than at any time in the past century. The book applies insights from psychoanalysis to provide a deeper awareness and understanding of the experience of these endings.

This work is useful and applicable to those experiencing, anticipating, or recovering from organisational death. Professionals working inside an organisation to help smooth the closure process would be strengthened by an understanding of the machinations of loss below the surface. Consultants brought in from the outside to plan and support closure could use these findings to open discussion and structure and facilitate closure.

Change is often embraced as certain and positive, it is assumed to be a good thing: if things were not to change for the better, then there would be no reason for change (Stapley & Roberts, 2000). This positive approach to change conceals the pain and vulnerability evoked by change and loss. This pain and suffering is often overlooked in the march forward towards reinvention. All change is loss, and all loss must be mourned (Levinson et al., 1962). The positive attitude evinced by the change culture is actually a denial of the loss that change creates.

This is an important topic of discussion at a time when organisational endings are part of so many people's worklife experience. Yet, despite endings being so commonplace, they are very easy to overlook.

Damien Hirst's 1991 pickled shark, titled *The Physical Impossibility of Death in the Mind of Someone Living*, captures visually the struggle faced in confronting our mortality, identified by Freud. This artwork, commissioned in 1991, is iconic and a symbol of Britart worldwide. The shark is symbolic of the giants of the financial sector, fierce conquerors, feared and admired in equal measure. The shark is made useless, a subject that becomes an object, almost a figure of derision. What was vital and terrifying has become still and tame. So, too, the bankers who commanded respect and admiration following the crisis became derided "wankers", objects of derision, scorn, and even pity.

Death and the City offers a psychoanalytic perspective of death in organisations. It brings fresh insight to Freud's work on death and applies this thinking to understand contemporary organisational closure and collapse. The book provides an in-depth portrait of an organisation in a palliative state. In this work, I transport the concepts of mourning and melancholia and of the death drive into the workplace and bring this important (but under-explored) stream of psychoanalytic thought to the fore as a means of interrogating and further understanding organisational life.

These concepts are illustrated through the results of a longitudinal study, based in a bank in the heart of the City of London that uses psychoanalytic observation and in-depth interviews to understand closure. I develop a framework that applies classical psychoanalytic theory, Freud, object relations theory, Klein, and Bion to organisational death. The self as a research tool is integral to this work, making sense of the closure by making sense of the self (Jervis, 2009).

The reader will gain an understanding of the experience and catastrophe of loss in the context of the global financial crisis. The pain of a slow corporate death and the acceptance of failure is illuminated using psychoanalytic theory helpful to consultants and academics dealing with endings. This book offers an original and in-depth understanding of organisational closure: the inner world of the organisation seen through the inner world of the researcher.

Eros and Thanatos

Neither the sun nor death can be looked at steadily. *"Le soleil ni la mort ne se peuvent regarder fixement"* (Maxim 26. Reflections, or Sentences and Moral Maxims (Françoise de la Rouchefoucauld (1665–1678)).

Death has the air of an indelicate subject. It is mentioned under one's breath, lowering the tone of one's voice. It is given deferential treatment. This cautious and tentative treatment of death extends to organisational life. Failure is not an option examined in the strategising of an organisation's future. Bankruptcy, bust, broke, or collapse are not pleasant words or associations to aspire to or to describe organisations. Yet, organisational collapse is part of our vernacular. Enron, Woolworths, Rover, BOAC, British Home Stores, Arthur Anderson, Parmalat, Barings Bank—these failures are part of our cultural experience of work.

Death is not looked at directly in Western culture, but through a filter. We do not have experience of our own death and an engagement with our mortality can be traumatic, but organisational death is something that can be experienced. The instinct towards life, Eros, and towards destruction, Thanatos, is examined here in the context of working life. The unpredictability of working life and the absence of lifetime institutions forces us to confront our occupational mortality. I offer an analysis of an organisation close to death and present a framework to apply psychoanalytic thought to future organisational endings.

The work deals with death, but also with dying, and explores the consequences of an anticipated death. The reason for organisational collapse is not central here; it is, rather, an exploration of the experience of those participating in that collapse and the lessons that can be learnt from such an examination. As an empirically driven study of organisational ending presented through a psychoanalytic lens, it brings a fresh perspective, using Freudian theory to provide useful insights and theoretical outputs that can be applied beyond the confines of the research organisation for closing and downsizing organisations. In short, it brings mourning and melancholia and the death drive to work.

Ways to read this book

The book is a combination of the results of an in-depth piece of research and an exploration of psychoanalytic theory associated with death and organisations. After the introductory chapter, Chapters Two and Three focus on "Death in Theory". For those keen to understand the theoretical underpinnings of the research, these provide that foundation. If your interest is in the substance of the research, then Chapters Four to Seven provide this. Chapter Eight concludes by pulling together all strands of the book.

The organisation presented has been renamed Interbank and New Interbank to protect the identity of the bank in question. However, the findings can be applied to numerous banks that collapsed or suffered during the financial crisis and, indeed, to any organisation facing downsizing, merger, or death.

Man is like a mere breath, his days are like a passing shadow

Psalm 144:4

CHAPTER ONE

Introducing death and the city

This introductory chapter makes the case for an examination of organisational death at a time when working lives are often vulnerable and organisational mortality is under threat from technology and the economy. It introduces the organisation, Interbank, and places the research at the heart of this book in the historical context of the global financial crisis and in the City of London. It focuses on the particular plight of a financial institution, post the 2008 financial crisis, but has relevance and application beyond both the institution and the market. Psychoanalysis, as a tool to deepen our understanding of organisation dynamics and organisational death, is explored.

Organisational death

Death is a subject that absorbs, provokes, and fascinates. There are those with experience of dying, chronicling the journey towards death, for example, Gould (2011), or those observing death (Lakotta & Schels, 2004). This book faces death and looks directly at the experience of collapse, endings, and closure. It employs human mortality as a metaphor for organisational ending: the individuals within the system continued to breathe and to function, yet the body of the organisation expired.

Organisational collapse is a feature of our everyday experience and the vulnerability of working life is visceral. This is not only in the financial sector, which has suffered deeply and visibly through the 2008 crash and beyond, but also in most other sectors: retail, property, professional services, manufacturing, and the public sector. Working prospects have changed with the loss of lifetime career expectations and the birth of the short lifespan organisation, creating an absence of security and safety. Mortal death and organisational death share a great deal. I do not purport that the end of an organisation is the end of a living, breathing organism, but that the end of an organisation has an impact on those in and around it in similar ways to the impact of an individual's death on those close to the deceased. Therefore, it shares a great deal with human death.

Organisations are operating in an environment where crises, failure, and demise are everyday features. Closure, merger, downsizing, redundancy, liquidation, insolvency, administration—this is the dialect of organisational life in a recession-driven economy. The economic and fiscal issues that lead to organisational mortality are accepted and, to a degree, understood; what is less understood is how the death process unfolds (Hansson, 2008). The exploration of death and loss at work has, however, had attention from Sievers (1994), who purports that organisations prevent its members from facing death; so preoccupied are they with the rigours of work, they are not equipped to deal with mortality. Stein (2009) and De Gooijer (2009) focus on downsizing and merger, and examine the loss and damage as a result of a drive for productivity improvements and profit. This work agrees with Bell and Taylor (2011), who identify that an engagement with loss and grief can add meaning and understanding to working life, although, as argued by Hansson and Wigblad (2006), data from closing organisations are hard to "catch" as organisations disappear. This transient nature of a closing organisation is captured in this work.

The impact of working with vulnerability at an organisational and personal level can be profound and generate a response that primarily aims to defend the subject (Menzies Lyth, 1960). Certainty and optimism are rare commodities and the world of work is, therefore, faced across all sectors with the prospect of endings. Such endings can be experienced as a profound source of loss and suffering (Driver, 2007, 2009). In such a climate, I address the relevance of confronting death with a psychoanalytic lens and offer a framework to consider endings as an inevitable part of organisational life.

This is particularly so in the City of London and the financial sector, where the catastrophic losses of future and fortune have been played out so dramatically. Loss of fortune can be measured on the stock exchange by pounds, dollars, and assets lost, but human loss cannot be quantified so accurately. The price of the loss of face, of one's future career, of confidence, or of status are the losses collected in the debris of declining organisations; these are much harder to measure.

Thanatos, or the Freudian death drive, has held an important but overlooked place in the canon of psychoanalytic literature. While Eros, in all its vicissitudes, is analysed, reinvented, and applied, death talk has not excited a similar interest. In the world of work, the contribution of death in psychoanalysis to our understanding of organisational mortality has been further buried. Through its psychoanalytically orientated exploration of death at work and its application of the disregarded model to organisation studies, this work demonstrates that the resurrection of death in psychoanalysis is a worthwhile act.

So, there is an absence of lifetime institutions. Generations of families historically secure in anticipating their future in the pre-global manufacturing-led world of steel, locomotives, coal, and shipping are vulnerable. Some generations of families have not experienced work. Our relationship to work is less secure and more transient and this represents a loss that is worthy of attention and understanding, particularly in these times of global and political uncertainty. Freud's preoccupation with an internal force of dissolution captured in *Beyond the Pleasure Principle* (1920g) and the exploration of differing responses to loss in "Mourning and melancholia" (1917e), extended by Klein (1984b[1940]), provide us with a framework of thinking about organisational death.

Death is an opportunity for second thoughts, a chance to reflect on the life that was, the achievements, regrets, and the possibilities of that life. An organisation's demise is equally an opportunity for reflection.

Psychoanalysis as a tool

The research presented is rooted in psychoanalytic theory. Psychoanalysis is both theory and practice. Psychoanalysis as theory is the body of work derived from the writings of Sigmund Freud that assumes the existence of a dynamic unconscious. Psychoanalysis as practice refers to the clinical practice of analysand and psychoanalyst meeting on numerous occasions during one week over a sustained period of time. There are variations in psychoanalytic practice but all derive from Freud and assume that there are ideas and thoughts hidden from the conscious mind: ideas and thoughts that are brought to the surface through the practice of psychoanalysis.

Psychoanalysis represents a depth approach to understanding organisational life and this book applies a depth of analysis specifically to death at work. Psychoanalysis has wide exploratory power and huge potential to allow us to think afresh about organisations. It offers original insights: the most advanced and compelling conception of human subjectivity that any theoretical approach has to offer (Fotaki et al., 2012, p. 1105). Notions such as repression, first introduced by Freud and the buried impulse or idea that is held in our unconscious are fundamental to a deeper understanding of what is going on below the surface in a work setting. This process of repression is known as a defence mechanism. We hold this and other defence mechanisms very dear and struggle to let go of our particular practice of repression. This is why there is often great resistance to therapeutic input and change.

Psychoanalytic thought and contributions have been somewhat sidelined in organisational psychology and this work brings psychoanalytic insight to the forefront of our understanding of organisations. This book is written on the foundation that working life includes both conscious and unconscious tasks and that these work alongside each other. The interaction between the conscious and unconscious dynamics at work can be productive and effective, what could be described as sophisticated work behaviour (Bion, 1961), or these forces can be at loggerheads, creating stress, fear, anxiety, and great inefficiency. The premise, therefore, is that organisations are social systems that have elements of conscious activity and elements of unconscious activity (Gould et al., 2001).

In a field full of emotion, psychoanalytic understanding at work, particularly in relation to death, does bring a third dimension to thinking that acknowledges our complexity as human beings and allows for the possibility that what is being said is not necessarily what is meant and what is being done is not necessarily straightforward. This writing adopts a psychodynamic approach that concentrates on the human aspects of work and management as an alternative to the dominant reductionist philosophy that tends to dominate our education system and our analysis of work (Stapley, 2006). It does not reject quantitative analysis that certainly has its place in understanding organisational endings but focuses instead on the experience of downfall for which a psychodynamic approach has much to offer.

The research applied a method of enquiry that explored unconscious processes in the organisation, psychoanalytic observation. This is commonly known as a psychodynamic or psychosocial methodology (Hollway & Jefferson, 2000, 2012). The transference and countertransference experience were critical to the collection and analysis of the data. A psychoanalytic approach to understanding death at work offers a nuanced and deep understanding of the experience of life in a dying institution. Through the collective experience of loss and grief, we can access rich data that helps to give organisational understanding and meaning (Bell & Taylor, 2011).

Psychoanalysis has a significant contribution to make to the understanding of organisations and work, yet this contribution has not been maximised, it has opened but a small window into the world of organization and management (Fotaki et al., 2012, p. 1106). This is true of an exploration of organisation death where a detailed insider record of organisation closure, using Freudian theory, has not yet been applied. The importance of this research lies in its deep and detailed recording of the death of an organisation, from the inside. Its innovation is its application of Freudian theory to the case, with rich data emerging from the investigation.

The City

The boundaries of the "City" are as clearly defined as the primordial traditions associated with this well-known plot in the capital. Its status as the centre of global finance is ancient, a claim the City has made throughout the nineteenth and twentieth centuries. The City of London, or "The City", proclaims itself the world leader in international finance and business services. The "Square Mile", as it is commonly known, is seen as the commercial heart of Britain. Hundreds of thousands of people flock to the city to work, largely in the financial services sector. Its mythology is of a destination paved with gold, a place to make fortunes and to rub shoulders with the successful and powerful. However, the City today, while showing signs of recovery, retains a lingering taint despite its commercial success. In the shadow of the financial crises of 2008, "dirty" bankers with "fat cat" salaries rub alongside those sentenced corporations on death row. This taint has extended to public protests such as the 2011–2012 tent city encampment in front of St Paul's Cathedral, where objectors to economic inequality and the fragility of global financial systems took to the streets. More than a decade after the rumblings of the crisis began, the City is still recovering from the aftershock of its collapse.

The City is not a place of production or manufacturing, its product is elusive and intangible. Banking and finance are the backbone of the capitalist society of which the UK is part and no judgement is placed on that truth. However, the financial crises of 2008 changed the gilded status of the City and demonstrated the vulnerability of institutions that many felt were *Too Big to Fail* (Sorkin, 2009). There was a belief that certain banks were too important to the economy to collapse and confidence that these would be saved by the American government.

Some efforts have been made to understand the money and the crisis from a psychoanalytic perspective (Bennett, 2012; Long & Sievers, 2012). This research offers a further psychoanalytic examination of the consequences for those people who enter a culture of swagger, of over-confidence, and of saving face when their time in the City is condemned. Disruption and chaos arrived in the City of London in 2008; this financial crisis has been likened to the sudden reversal of a speeding car down an empty country lane, with the consequential explosion of the engine and vehicle to the point of no repair (Lanchaster, 2010).

This crash was equally unanticipated: institutions were thought of as invincible. This was a financial crisis that shook the world. Lehman Brothers filed for bankruptcy in September 2008 and the City of London joined the collapse.

Organisations can face many different endings—sharp and brutal, premature, or carefully planned and premeditated. The financial crisis of 2008 brought with it different types of organisational casualties. Some financial institutions were absorbed, such as Bank of America. Others closed dramatically and suddenly, such as Lehman's. The images of shocked City workers walking away from their shiny office buildings with cardboard boxes of belongings are iconic pictures of the crisis. Others, like the institution of this research, faced a certain but well planned and slow ending. Government assistance allowed the organisation time to tidy up and close down methodically and systematically. The impending death offered a fertile research space for this investigation.

The organisation: Interbank

The organisation examined was a financial institution that operated in the City but was headquartered outside of the UK. The institution was part of the financial boom and collapsed in 2008. It was taken over by a government body (unlike Lehman Brothers) but this rescue was merely palliative: the government intervention acted as an interim support, with the prospect of the organisation facing its own certain demise. The observation location for the duration of the research was in the heart of the City of London.

The research was empirically led and carried out at a critical time of change and recalibration in the financial capital of the City of London. The heady days of excess, profit, and extreme opportunity were over and the organisation at the heart of the research could certainly be described as a casualty of the financial crisis of 2008. However, until shortly before its collapse, it was notable as an inter-national darling of the financial markets. Whether the organisation was an innocent casualty or the perpetrator of its own demise is not deliberated.

The organisation's fall from grace was dramatic. Until the loans controversy surrounding the bank, this organisation was feted as an example of exemplary leadership, creativity, and success. This changed dramatically with multiple senior resignations, widespread media interest, public vilification of the leadership team, and survival ensured only by the nationalisation of the institution by a government body. This survival, however, would be short lived, with its existence guaranteed only for the period of closure and management of the debt book.

The environment in which the research was conducted was not, at first glance, fragile. The bank occupied several floors of a prestigious high-rise building in the heart of the City, the rigour of day to day office life was observed, with polished and efficient security guards protecting entry to the building. There were comfortable, even luxurious, surroundings, and a clean and modern office space. Previously, it had conducted itself internationally, with a presence in America, Asia, and Europe, dealing with business and commercial banking, wealth management, and property lending. The bank, as other financial institutions also experienced, was disparaged and broadly and loudly criticised for its perceived appalling failings. This animosity was expressed via social media, the press, television, and radio.

Throughout, I have withheld any further information about the organisation to protect its anonymity, as promised in order to gain entry.

DEATH IN THEORY

CHAPTER TWO

Death and psychoanalysis

The theoretical underpinning of this book is presented in this chapter through an exploration of death in psychoanalysis. Different psychoanalytic representations of loss, death, and endings are examined as a vehicle to further our understanding of organisational mortality. My emphasis will be on Freud and the fundamental place loss has in psychoanalytic literature, a place forced to one side by the popularisation of the erotic and the emphasis on love and desire. Psychoanalytic thought locates loss centrally: loss of the primal relationship, loss of memory, and denial of loss. This sense of loss has something to offer the world of work at a time of organisational ending. I present the challenge of confronting death and acknowledging the limitations of life. Freud's engagement with death in his writings on transience, war, and death are relevant here. War is important in any reflection on death: in war, one is confronted with the possibility of death from the outset; this is given attention and related to organisational death.

The development of the death drive, first introduced in *Beyond the Pleasure Principle* (1920g) and revisited in *Civilization and its Discontents* (1930a), is presented. The enigma of the death drive as both a return to nothingness and a force for destruction is explored. I present the ways in which death is managed through a detailed examination of "Mourning and melancholia", the 1917 paper at the root of object relations thinking, the work that examines normal and pathological responses to loss.

Death is evident in much of psychoanalysis; key texts address it directly, but death also runs through other psychoanalytic thought. Patricide features strongly in *Totem and Taboo* (1912–1913), a collection of four essays that give us Freud's first attempt to apply his theory to anthropology. Freud demonstrates here an interest in the impact of death on those left behind and cites the example of a deceased beloved relative being transformed into a demon at the moment of death. Here, also, the notion of primal slaughter, and the mark it has made on humanity, was put forward as one of Freud's bold notions.

The chapter is structured around the following themes.

(i)   The impossibility of death: the struggle of psychoanalytic thinking to acknowledge and address death as a valid field of psychoanalytic enquiry is studied.

(ii) Working through death: responses to endings, normal and pathological. The framing of death in this way orders the subject and relates to the findings from my research.

(iii) Nothingness *vs.* destruction: the oscillating elements of the death drive that swing between destruction and a return to nothingness.

(iv) Loss *vs.* desire: the priority given to desire and the erotic, balanced with the relevance and applicability of loss in psychoanalysis.

The impossibility of death

In "Thoughts for the time on war and death", Freud reflects that in the unconscious, every one of us is convinced of his own immortality (Freud, 1915b, p. 291). Freud purports that death is not a significant psychic factor and that fear of death is secondary. Death, asserts Freud, has no place in the unconscious and when we speak of the fear of death, we are really referring to something else. In the most simple of terms, Freud asserts death's absence from the mind (1915b, 1923b, 1926d). Freud describes death as an abstract, temporal issue that has no place in the unconscious; he states that there is no death in the unconscious *todesangst* (fear of death). The key challenge of psycho-analytic engagement with death is the impossibility of accepting our mortality. As we cannot experience death, or observe our death, death is something that cannot be held in the mind and, therefore, cannot be contemplated. Thus, Freud was quite dismissive of the importance and centrality of death in psychic thinking. "The high-sounding phrase, 'every fear is ultimately the fear of death', has hardly any meaning, and at any rate, cannot be justified" (Freud, 1923b, p. 57).

Yet, Freud's relationship with death was more complex than a denunciation of the significance of the fear of death, or of death anxi-ety. He oscillates between an outright rejection of death as having any psychic significance to a deep engagement with the subject. The side-stepping of death in psychoanalysis is seen by some as a lacuna, literally an act of repression (Razinsky, 2013). Freud's assertion that there is an absence of the psychic presence of death appears flawed. Freud's own experiences of loss—his diagnosis of cancer, his son's involvement in the war, the loss of his beloved daughter and grand-son—led Freud to write, "fundamentally everything has lost its meaning for me" (Letter quoted in Eissler, 1978, p. 229). Such senti-ments suggest that death is at the heart of psychic life, not on the side-lines.

Engaging with death

Not only is death something that is hard to engage with in relation to our own mortality, it is also a general topic for hushed tones and murmured consideration. Confronting mortality persists as a delicate subject. In Western society, this has been so for centuries. In the midst of the First World War, Freud encouraged us to bring death to the fore. "Would it not be better to give death the place in reality and in our thoughts that it is due and bring out our unconscious attitude to death, which we have hitherto suppressed, a little more?" (Freud, 1916a, p. 193).

However, Freud fails to respond to his own call to engage with the subject and maintains an arms-length treatment of death, despite the preoccupation with death evident in his personal life and correspon-dence (Fliess, 1899, in Freud, 1985). In "On transience" (1916a), Freud explores the interference of anticipated death on one's ability to live and embrace life.

> Not long ago I went on a summer walk through a smiling countryside in the company of a taciturn friend and of a young but already famous poet. The poet admired the beauty of the scene around us but felt no joy in it. He was disturbed by the thought that all this beauty was fated to extinction, that it would vanish when winter came, like all human beauty and all the beauty and splendour that men have created or may create. All that he would otherwise have loved and admired seemed to him to be shorn of its worth by the transience which was its doom. (Freud, 1916a, p. 303)

Here, the capacity to mourn is explained as crucial to appreciation of life itself. Our mortality allows us to value beauty and to value the moment. Living on the edge, the excitement and thrill of life at the heart of the financial world provides energy and risk associated with working life in the City of London. This is central to its appeal and, perhaps, central also to the creativity and ecstasy of success. Yet, it is also possible that, caught up in the demands of the City, there is little opportunity to look around and appreciate the satisfaction in that work, perhaps until the time that it is no longer available. Life is beautiful, but life is short, appears to be the motif of Freud's 1916 piece. This is a sentiment with which the workers in the City in 2008 might well have concurred.

Freud on war and death

War plays an important part in any reflection on death because the possibility of death is present from the outset. It encompasses the sacrifice of one's life for a greater good, be that country, battalion, value, or philosophy. It is war that raises the question of how our unconscious responds to the problem of the dead. This question remains worthy of investigation a century later. Death of the object might be a loved one, a home, or an object of attachment of any kind. In the case of this research, the loss refers to the loss of the organisation to which one once belonged and in which one was employed.

Freud ponders life and death in "Thoughts for the times on war and death" (1915b). In this paper, he considers war and death in two parts, "The disillusion of war" and "Our attitude towards death" (1915b). In the first part, "The disillusion of war", Freud uses the space to muse on difference, the joy of freedom to move from one "father-land" to another, to enjoy blue and grey sea. He laments the lack of understanding between great nations and the turning against each other with venom and hatred. The representation of the people by states and governments casts a dark shadow and deems individuals defenceless against the grim rumour or situation.

> So well may the civilized cosmopolitan whom I introduced above stand helplessly in this world that has now grown strange to him, his great fatherland collapsed, the common possessions ruined, his fellow citizens divided and degraded. (Freud, 1915b, p. 174)

Freud offers some critical remarks about the "cosmopolitan's" dis-illusion, the disillusion of war that rests on two key elements: brutal-ity, and a lack of morality. Illusions are recommended to us by the fact that they spare feelings of displeasure and allow us to enjoy satis-factions in their place. We must then accept it without complaint if, at some point, they collide with a piece of reality upon which they shatter (Freud, 1915b, p. 174). The morality of a good or evil person is presented against the well-versed Freudian notion that all people are subject to the same drives or impulses: at this stage, Freud has not developed the death instinct. Primitive impulses go through a lengthy process of development and in the emergence of a person's character. Moral standards have been forced high in response to civil obedience, demands of good conduct do not pay heed to man's instinctual foun-dations. Therefore, continues Freud, our pain and disillusion at the uncivilised behaviour of war are unjustified, as they are based on an illusion: man has not fallen so far, man has merely not risen as high as had been imagined. Such reference to idealisation is relevant later in analysing the response of employees to the collapse of their "civil-isation". Freud refers us again to dreams, to the freedom to return to our instinctual state in our sleep. "Every day it [psychoanalysis] is able to show that the keenest-minded people will suddenly behave without insight, like idiots, once the required insight encounters an emotional resistance in them" (Freud, 1916a, p. 181).

Freud ends this essay tentatively. He refers to the mystery of the hatred of one people for another, one nation for another, even in peacetime. He suggests that perhaps, once all moral inhibitions are removed, what we are left with is the most brutal of psychical attitudes and only later in our evolution might we be able to do something to transform this regrettable state of affairs. According to Freud, the hero is not one who confronts death and faces it with courage, but the opposite. For the hero who puts his life in danger there is no sense of mortality; he sees himself as literally immortal. In risking death, he is not facing death, but ignoring death. The game of life is actually of no value, for in his mind there can always be a rematch (Razinsky, 2013).

The second part of the essay, "Our attitude towards death" (1915b), begins by saying that our attitude is not honest, that we outwardly purport the inevitability of death, yet we behave as if we are immortal: "We have shown the unmistakable tendency to push death aside, to eliminate it from life" (Freud, 1915b, p. 183). No matter how much we contemplate our own death, we are always onlookers on that possibility and so, argues Freud, the unconscious is convinced of its immortality. The subject of another's death, writes Freud, is not something that is discussed in the hearing of the person who is about to die; only children appear to contradict this unwritten law of confronting another person's death directly. This delicate treatment of death continues post death itself, where the custom is not to speak ill of the dead: *De mortuis nil nisi bonum* (Freud, 1915b, p. 184).

This attitude towards death, suggests Freud, has huge bearing on how we live our lives, and, indeed, has an impoverishing effect in that we are paralysed by the fear of death and so limit our lifetime activities, resorting instead to the arts and literature for the thrill of life. War means that this attitude towards death cannot be maintained, as large numbers of deaths are occurring day after day. Primeval man's attitude to death was different, deduces Freud. Death was taken seriously, on the one hand, in consideration of the daily dangers of survival faced in primitive life. However, on the other hand, death was also embraced by man. War brings primeval man back to the surface.

The paper ends with an old proverb: "*Si vis pacem, para bellum*. If you wish to preserve peace, arm for war", and the suggestion that this might be the time to replace it to read as follows: "*Si vis vitam, para mortem*. If you wish to endure life, prepare yourself for death" (Freud, 1915b, p. 194). This work appears several years before *Beyond the*

Pleasure Principle (1920g) is published, but sows the seeds of the death instinct. This writing is Freud's first direct examination of the mortal subject.

Freud in correspondence with Einstein, 1933: "Why war?"

Freud's thoughts on death developed in the years leading up to the Second World War. In anticipation of the eventuality of another war, these two great minds exchanged thoughts on war and death. The exchange of letters between Einstein and Freud in 1932 (published in 1933) provides an insight into Freud's despair at war. He almost seems to have run out of things to say when he writes, "In your letter you yourself had said most of what needed to be said on the subject. You had, so to speak, taken the wind out of my sails, but I am happy to drift in your wake" (Freud, 1933b, p. 221). Freud's letter muses on the nature of war and responds to questions raised by Einstein on the nature of man's attraction to aggression and power. This piece also clearly shows the development of his thinking around the death drive and succinctly outlines his theory of man's drive to return to his inanimate self. There seems to be agreement between them about the ease with which man is roused to war: Einstein refers to a drive to hate and to destroy, Freud shows his agreement and takes the opportunity to explain drive theory:

> According to our hypothesis, man's drives are of two kinds only, those which seek to preserve and unite—we call erotic, exactly in the sense in which Plato uses the world Eros in his *Symposium*, or sexual, with a deliberate over-extension of the popular conception of sexuality— and others which seek to destroy and kill; we sum these up as the drive to aggression or the drive to destruction. (Freud, 1933b, p. 227)

He relates this polarity with the polarity of attraction and repulsion of Einstein's discipline; he reminds Einstein of the countless cruelties that bear witness to man's pleasure in destruction and aggression. Freud brings violence to the fore as a more accurate and less delicate use of power. He writes here of war in a way that can be applied equally well to organisational life:

> This, I think gives us all the essentials; the overcoming of violence by the transfer of power to the greater entity, held together by the emotional bonds of its members. All else is merely an enactment and repetition. Relations remain simple as long as the community consists only of a number of equally strong individuals. (Freud, 1933b, p. 223)

Not all wars are seen as the same. Some bring disaster; through others there is a transformation of violence into law, thereby abolishing violence and bringing a new legal order. Freud disavows the existence of a peaceful nation where compulsion and aggression are not known and pursues his description of drive theory by offering Eros as an opposing force to the drive to destruction. The creation of emotional bonds with a love-object, sometimes, but not always, sexual, and the relationship with a love-object through identification should surely work against war. Why he asks, do we rage about war and not accept it as one of life's hardships? He answers his own question with the explanation that all human beings have the right to life, a right for a hope-filled life that war destroys. Freud pursues his description of the death drive, at work in every living creature, at work to bring life back to a state of inanimate material.

> The death-drive becomes the drive to destruction, when it is applied externally, against objects, with the help of certain organs. The organism preserves its own life, so to speak, by destroying that which is strange to it. But a certain part of the death-drive remains active within the living creature, and we have attempted to derive a whole number of normal and pathological phenomena from this internalization of the drive to destruction. (Freud, 1933b, p. 228)

Freud brought the death drive to fruition after the experience and exposure to death following the devastating consequences of the First World War. The state of nothingness and relief from all tension would be desirable, literally a state of perfect rest (Frosh, 2012).

Through the financial crises of 2008 and the ensuing recession and double dip recession, the world of work has faced its own war zone. Loss of livelihood, career progression, and future has been widespread and changed the landscape of organisational life. This seems a particularly pertinent time to apply the significance of the death drive to work at a time when the desire to be removed from all stimulation and tension might well be at its peak.

Working through death

This part of the chapter deals with responses to loss and ways of working through death presented in the psychoanalytic literature. Before his pronouncement of the death drive, Freud explores mourning and melancholia in his 1917 essay that tackles the human response to loss. He writes of the process of loss and mourning and uses an investigation of pathological responses to loss to help us understand what is, indeed, normal. This piece of writing is hugely important to the development of psychoanalytic thought and introduces object relations theory. Freud sets out to clarify the difference between mourning and melancholia.

What Freud referred to as melancholia is most akin to contemporary depression (Leader & Corfield, 2008). Melancholia was interpreted and reserved by others for the most psychotic and extreme forms of depression (Laplanche, 1970). This perhaps contributes to Laplanche's rejection of the death drive as a viable psychoanalytic tool.

Mourning and melancholia

Although these states of mourning and melancholia are often triggered by the same circumstances, Freud discusses what conditions need to be present for the two states to progress along their varying paths. While some statements are based on observations, much of his writing on melancholia is conjectured, and Freud continues to remind the reader of this by asking questions of his own theories throughout the essay. He extends mourning beyond the loss of a loved person to the loss of an object, some abstraction that had taken the place of one, such as one's country, liberty, an ideal, and so on (Freud, 1917e, p. 243). It is the extension of loss beyond the loved person to the loss experienced at work and through work that is at the heart of this book.

Mourning is described as a normal reaction to events and one that is carried through with the passage of time. It is not, therefore, associated with pathological issues. During the mourning period, the person realises that the loved person or object that is lost is truly gone and turns away from reality. This turning away from reality is marked by dejection, loss of interest, inability to love, and inhibition of all activities. These same symptoms are present in melancholia; however, in mourning, the reality of loss and absence is eventually recognised and, over time, the mourner returns to his or her normal state, but the melancholic cannot separate from the lost object and turns inwards, complaints become "plaints". The melancholic turns on himself and blames himself: he is at fault, and should have seen the end coming.

Melancholic self-accusations can be turned against the lost object (in the case of this research, the failed organisation) with anger and outrage at the injustice. In the shattering of object-relationship, mourning focuses on the lost object, and with melancholia the focus is on the abandonment of the relationship. The melancholic is constantly seeking the lost object and trying to find where it is located. Mourning is, thus, described as a conscious response to something, a specific death, whereas melancholia is more to do with the unconscious, resulting from a loss that cannot be physically perceived, like love. It is worth noting that Freud makes this distinction. It is a bizarre claim that such a profound event as even so-called "normal mourning" has no unconscious content. Thus, melancholia is more puzzling because of this absence of a loss that can be observed, and there also exists the additional symptom of a lowering of self-regard. "In mourning it is the world which has become poor and empty; in melancholia it is the ego itself" (Freud, 1917e, p. 246).

The person believes that he is inferior and despicable and cannot imagine a time when he has not been repugnant; the melancholic is comfortable in sharing the truth about his awful self. This marks melancholy as a different symptom from inferiority complexes that are buried and have associations of shame. Melancholia is like an open wound, a prolonged injury, even unending. Yet, the melancholic could be described as comfortable in his position; his attack is focused on the lost object rather than on himself.

The disturbance of self-regard

Freud describes the healthy response to loss—mourning—as differing in one fundamental regard to the pathological response to loss—melancholia. That difference is the lowering of self-regard and self-repulsion. ". . . a lowering of the self-regarding feelings to a degree that finds utterance in self-reproaches and self-revilings, and culminates in a delusional expectation of punishment" (Freud, 1917e, p. 244).

Within the organisational context of a failing business, one can map such feelings of self-reproach on those who blame themselves for the downfall of their place of work. If only I had worked harder, or won that contract, or raised my concerns or brought in more business—perhaps then the business would have survived. There are elements of narcissism in such self-reproach, a means of expanding the importance of one's own contribution to the success or failure of the entire organisation.

Object-loss transformed into ego-loss

The attack on the self becomes interesting as the paper develops. Here, Freud dissects the violent self-accusations and concludes that these attacks are not necessarily on the person himself, but that they do fit very closely the image of someone else, the image of the person who has been lost. So, the accusations that the melancholic directs inwards are unconsciously attacks on the loved object that has been lost. The emotional response to the loss is outrage, disappointment, and anger. Thus, if we relate the previous self-accusations away from the person concerned, the individual working in the condemned organisation, and direct them instead towards the organisation itself, the attack is different.

Instead of, if only I had worked harder, or won that contract, the attack is towards the organisation: if only the organisation was better structured to win contracts and reward hard work, we might have survived. Rather than reproaches of, if only I had raised my concerns, we might hear, if only the business had behaved ethically. Instead of, if only I had brought in more business, the attack might be turned on the decision makers who could be accused of not producing the right product, or price plan, so that then the business would have survived. Blame, attack, and accusation shifted from oneself to the organisation as a whole, relieving the burden of one's responsibility for the success or failure of the entire organisation. Yet, it is vital to remember that such mental states are not conscious and the internal voice of the individual who defines himself as repugnant, unworthy, and to blame is being driven by his unconscious and not his thinking, logical self. The melancholic never explicitly reproaches the object, but only indirectly, through his self-reproaches. An attack on the organisation would, therefore, not be characteristic of the melancholic, who would direct his reproaches inwards rather than blaming the organisation.

One unconscious part of the ego stalking another

It is important to stress that both mourning and melancholia are applicable to situations that extend far beyond the death of a loved one or close friend. Symptoms of loss can be extended beyond the death of a human being to the loss of relationship, object, or fantasy. This is the premise of this research: that the work on mourning and melancholia has a contribution to the loss experienced as a result of organisational closure.

> In melancholia, the occasions which give rise to the illness extend for the most part beyond the clear case of a loss by death, and include all those situations of being slighted, neglected or disappointed, which can import opposed feelings of love and hate in the relationship or reinforce an already existing ambivalence ... (Freud, 1917e, p. 251)

The forces of love and hate that are a feature of internal object relations are also a feature of pathological relationships such as an abusive partnership or an abused child—the experience of loving hate and hateful love. This is perhaps the most uncomfortable element to trace to organisational life, where sadistic behaviour is regularly evidenced.

The psychotic edge of mania and melancholia

Freud provides another layer of meaning to melancholia by describing the way in which melancholia can switch to mania, whereby mania triumphs in overcoming the painful feelings that crush the melancholic. Freud uses the extended metaphor of the analyst as detective to explain the way in which melancholia can transform into mania. He describes mania and melancholia wrestling with the same unconscious complex: in melancholia, the ego has succumbed and been consumed by the painful and crushing loss, and in mania, the pain has been pushed aside. Freud attempts to explain the exuberance and triumph experienced in mania using a vignette of a "poor wretch" who wins a great deal of money. In winning the money, the individual is relieved of everyday worries and concerns. Freud also talks of the situation when, after an arduous struggle, one is finally crowned with success. Ogden suggests this must surely relate to his own wish to have his contribution and status recognised (Ogden, 2012).

The wish to continue living and the wish to be at one with the dead

Ambivalence is presented as an unconscious expression of unresolved feeling of love and hate, as might be seen in a healthy oedipal experience or the torment of an obsessional neurotic (Ogden, 2012). However, in the case of mourning and melancholia, ambivalence is presented as a different struggle, that of a wish to be at one with the living and a wish to be at one with the dead.

> In melancholia the relation to the object is no simple one; it is complicated by the conflict due to ambivalence. The ambivalence is either constitutional, i.e. is an element of every love-relation formed by this particular ego, or else it proceeds precisely from those experiences that involved the threat of losing the object. For this reason, the exciting causes of melancholia have a much wider range than those of mourning, which is for the most part occasioned only by a real loss of the object, by its death. (Freud, 1917e, p. 255)

How can this concept of ambivalence be directed towards one's experience of working in a dying organisation? Here, there is strong evidence that identity attachment and evaluation of self is strongly tied to working identity. Gratitude for the career opportunity and exposure might be mixed with resentment of loss of future and taint associated with working in an organisation that is closing down (Bell & Taylor, 2011; Kahn & Liefooghe, 2014).

Some question the validity of extending clinical accounts of melancholia to social theory (Frosh, 2012). Yet, there are signs that this use of psychoanalysis, for example in applying the metaphor of post-colonial melancholy, is helpful and powerful (Khanna, 2004), or in using a psychoanalytic lens to understand the desire for whiteness (Seshadri-Crooks, 2000).

The fundamental elements of Freud's writing on mourning and melancholia explain the unconscious, organised around stable internal object relations. This thinking can be very powerful and cut off dialogue between the unconscious internal world and the real external objects. Love and hate are bound together with external object relationships replaced by an unconscious, internal, fantasised object relationship. This can be an effective defence against psychic pain. It is not just love and hate that are bound together, but also the wish to be one with one's object relationships and at one with one's dead internal objects.

> In this way the shadow of the object fell upon the ego, which could now be condemned by a particular agency as an object, as the abandoned object. Thus the loss of object had been transformed into a log of ego, and the conflict between the ego and the beloved person into a dichotomy between ego-criticism and the ego as modified by identification. (Freud, 1917e, p. 209)

The unconscious conflict of love and hate presents one version of ambivalence in Freud's early writing, but, in "Mourning and melancholia", he uses it in a different way, to express a wish to be at one with the living and at one with the dead. There is a choice in this ambivalence between the wish to be alive, with the pain of irreversible loss, and the reality of death and the wish to be free of the pain of loss and the knowledge of death (Ogden, 2012). The mourner is able to free himself from this struggle and chooses to live. The melancholic is caught in the constant struggle between the two.

It is here that we can best understand the relationship between mourning and melancholia and the death instinct. Although the latter does not present itself formally until 1920, its roots are clearly evident in these offerings. The death instinct draws us to a position where we are free from all pain, all loss, and all suffering. We return to the ultimate inorganic state where there is no fear, no knowledge, and no suffering.

Melancholia is described as deriving some of its characteristics from mourning and the rest from narcissism. The loss of the loved object turns into pathological mourning, forcing self-reproach and self-blame for the loss of the loved object.

> If the love of the object, which cannot be abandoned while the object itself is abandoned, has fled into narcissistic identification, hatred goes to work on this substitute object, insulting it, humiliating it, making it suffer and deriving a sadistic satisfaction from that suffering. (Freud, 1917e, p. 211)

The pleasure of self-torment evidenced in melancholia suggests the satisfaction of tendencies towards sadism and hatred. The hatred is applied to the lost person and then turned back on against the melancholic.

Klein's engagement with death and envy

Of those that came after Freud, the thinker with one of the greatest engagements with death is Melanie Klein. Klein, and the Kleinians who followed her, for example, Segal (1958) and Jaques (1988), place death centrally; it is seen as major force in psychic life and at the heart of our anxieties. For Klein, Freud has not placed death anxiety in the primary position it deserves (1948): for her, death anxiety is our foremost and deepest anxiety.

> Anxiety has its origin in the fear of death; if we assume the existence of a death instinct, we must also assume that in the deepest layers of the mind there is a response to this instinct in the form of fear of annihilation of life. . . . the danger arising from the inner working of the death instinct is the first cause of anxiety. (Klein, 1948, p. 116)

The death instinct embraced and developed by Klein (1984b[1940]) does, however, take root in Freud's writing on mourning and melancholia and the way in which a lost object is internalised and both idealised and vilified. This tension creates an inability for normal reparative processes to occur. This festering and inability to separate from the lost object creates the melancholic stance. In this stance, thinking from a depressive position is impossible. From such a position, suicide can be viewed as murder by proxy, in other words, murder of the internalised object.

Klein's work in the object relations tradition is steeped in loss. Her concept of the infant's loss of the good object (the breast and milk) and the destructive phantasies and impulses against the mother's breasts as a result of the infant's greed and destruction of the source of goodness is the first relation to an other. Klein depicts the depressive position as a process of early "reality testing" and argues that this is a classic form of what will later become the process of mourning (1984b[1940]). Klein sees psychic conflict not as a pull between the ego and the drives, but between the life drive and the death drive, with anxiety as the response to the death drive, the basis of persecutory anxiety observed in young children (1952). In Klein, we find mania's triumph over the lost object.

Klein's theoretical contribution of the paranoid–schizoid position can be seen to derive directly from the death drive. This was pivotal to her work and her contribution to psychoanalytic thought. She proposed this basic destructive drive at work in each individual (the death drive) with projection and splitting defensive processes developed to protect the ego against the death drive. Klein's structural notions of projective identification and the paranoid–schizoid and depressive positions were based on fundamental Freudian concepts. Projective identification develops and builds on Freud's ideas of projection. It can be understood as the unconscious projection of unwanted aspects of oneself into others. In this way, desired and undesired aspects of the self can be split off (Klein, 1946) and the individual can be bolstered. The theory rests on the assumption that there are conflicting elements of self that co-exist; when it becomes unbearable to own elements of the self, these unbearable elements can be projected into others.

Klein formulated the paranoid–schizoid position in 1946, although she does posit splitting, part-objects and fantasised attacks in the pre-depressive infant. The first stage in infantile development presented a developmental stage in structural thinking. The movement between paranoid–schizoid and depressive positions explained the shift from psychotic to healthy psychological functioning. The depressive position, often described as elusive, allows the integration of whole object, integrating love and hate.

Her concepts of these moveable states, the fluidity between the paranoid–schizoid and depressive positions, proved highly applicable to clinical work as well to organisational work. The life enhancing and life destructive forces Klein describes mingle equally in the corporate world. Her belief in the temporary stability of such states, threatened from external and internal sources, seem particularly applicable to organisational life in a condemned institution.

Klein's theory on death is closely linked to envy. Her publication of *Envy and Gratitude* (1957) came towards the end of her theoretical contributions and it has been argued that this is why this important contribution is sometimes overlooked (Stein, 2000). Klein describes envy as the destructive feelings evoked by the knowledge that someone else possesses or enjoys something desirable. Accompanying such feelings is the wish to destroy or spoil that object. Klein viewed envy as a painful affliction, oral and sadistic in nature.

Klein's shift from the Freudian oedipal triangle (mother, father, and child) to the pre-oedipal dyad (mother and child) focused on dramas of love and hate. She herself was at the heart of much antimony and drama from Freudians who viewed her work as revisionist (Cohen, 2005). Klein sees the root of envy in the early stages of life, when the infant directs envious attacks towards the feeding breast, and then later towards parental coitus. The attack on the good object is seen as a manifestation of primary destructiveness, a challenge to the depressive position integration and the expression of love (the latter she describes as gratitude). Klein attributed enormous significance to the first year of life, more than childhood as a whole, and, in this fundamental way, she and Freud differed. In this early period of development, Klein saw the death instinct as a purely destructive force, a force that induces anxiety about disintegration and about annihilation (Carr & Lapp, 2006); seen in this way, envy emerges as a significant expression of the death instinct.

Nothingness vs. destruction

If we are to take it as a truth that knows no exception that everything living dies for *internal* reasons—becomes inorganic once again—then we shall be compelled to say that '*the aim of all life is death*' and, looking backwards, that '*inanimate things existed before living ones*'. (Freud, 1920g, p. 38)

Freud was interested in the earlier state of things, that which preceded life and would be restored in death. Human beings are nudged into life and change; Freud proposes that there is resistance to change and progress and, as we have just examined, a wish to return to death. He writes, "It seems, then, that an instinct is an urge inherent in organic life to restore an earlier state of things" (Freud, 1920g, p. 36).

Compulsion to repeat

In *Beyond the Pleasure Principle*, Freud introduces us to the repetitive play of his grandchild, who, in a game of *fort* (gone) and *da* (there), attempts to master his separation from his mother. The pain of his mother's separation, and choice to be without the child, is played out in this game, a representation of this everyday catastrophe (Cohen, 2005, p. 106). The compulsion to repeat our existing behaviour acts as a highly effective barrier to allowing insights into our unconscious (Freud, 1920g). Freud questioned whether we would find the courage to recognise the existence of a compulsion to repeat, one that overrides the pleasure principle and drives our wish to return. It is almost as if he is thinking aloud, offering us a return to our most basic desires and a wish to repeat those basic conditions.

For Freud, instincts uncover an effort to return to an earlier state of things: using biology as a starting point, with embryology and bird migration cited as examples in nature, he brings us the compulsion to repeat (Freud, 1933a). In the analytic context, repressed and forgotten incidences of childhood are repeated through dreams and associations. Counter to the pleasure principle, these repeated incidences are often of a disturbing and painful nature. The "daemonic" character of the compulsion to repeat is not restricted to the analytic situation, but appears in the repetition of doomed relationships, friendships, and encounters (Freud, 1920g).

In repetition, or acting out, there is a resistance to remembering. This manifests itself in the consulting room by a patient who might not identify defiance in his relationship to his parents but, instead, brings that defiance to the consulting room and to the analyst (Freud, 1914g). Analysts refer to a period of "working through" to apply to the period of time it takes a patient to absorb the insight into the nature and function of their defensive behaviour. This extends beyond a patient's conscious decision to relinquish such behaviours. For this work, it is argued that the acting out and working through occurs also in the workplace.

Change involves letting go of attachment to objects, be they lost loved ones or familiar patterns of behaviour, and existing in a new and changed form. Repetition compulsion was also used by Freud in support of the theory of the death instinct. Our innate tendency to revert to primitive conditions links the death drive to the life drive. The animate drive emerges from the inanimate drive and the death drive calls for a return to this inanimate state.

Freud, therefore, did not dismiss the importance of sexual drives, but introduced another drive, one that takes away all tension, pain, and unwanted stimulation, a drive towards a state of death. The potential for self-destruction within humankind has given the death drive something of a controversial nature. It has been warmly embraced by some psychoanalysts, notably Klein (1984b[1940]), although she imbues it with a different meaning.

The death drive

Our views have from the very first been *dualistic,* and to-day they are even more definitely dualistic than before—now that we describe the opposition as being, not between ego-instincts and sexual instincts but between life instincts and death instincts. (Freud, 1920g, p. 53)

If Freud's first point of reference is the Oedipus complex, then the second is the death drive (Carr & Lapp, 2006; Weatherill, 1999). The death drive is part of Freud's second topographical model. The first topography postulated the dynamic unconscious world with associated drives and anxieties based on infantile sexual experience. Sexual drives remained important to Freud but his second topography included the development of the death drive: a drive that compels living creatures to strive for a lifeless, inorganic state. Thanatos, or the death instinct, as the death drive is also commonly referred to (Rycroft, 1995), is not an aggressive or destructive instinct against others; rather, it turns that instinct in on itself so that, instead of wishing to annihilate the other, the drive is to annihilate oneself and to return to a state of nothing—literally, to dissolve.

However, Freud does not speak of Thanatos in substantive terms; he was wary of it and did not see it as having its own energy. Eros (love) takes the death drive into itself and renders it invisible. The death drive is a return to life's purest form. Freud introduced the concept of the death drive as a negative concept in opposition to the drive for life.

So, while Eros is paired with the energy of "libido", Thanatos has no such equivalent energy beyond a suggested name "mortido destrudo" (Rycroft, 1995).

Freud, in *Beyond the Pleasure Principle* (1920g), shares the idea that death is no longer an easy option. External influences make death more difficult and an organism has to make many detours and take circuitous routes before reaching death. Dollimore describes life itself as only a detour to death (2001, p. 186). This captures what is difficult to grasp in understanding the death drive. Freud describes a falling back into complete satisfaction, a return to the fundamental of living organisms to death. It is the nature of social and psychic life that, rather than falling back, we are compelled to move forward, as the "backward path" is blocked by repressions on which society is built.

The most fundamental repression in Freudian terms is the blocking of desire; the containment of libidinal freedom is the basis of civilisation. Yet, if this seems a contradiction of the foundation of the Freudian principles of Eros and the libido, it should be noted that Freud makes a crucial exception in this drive towards death: "Instinctual life as a whole serve [sic] to bring about death . . . apart from the sexual instincts" (Freud, 1920g, p. 311, cited in Dollimore, 2001, p. 187).

Schopenhauer (1966[1819]) should be recognised as a proponent of the death drive before Freud. Dying, decreed Schopenhauer, should be regarded as the real aim of life. Although described as anticipating Freud, Freud, although acknowledging his contribution, claims only to have read him later in life and is, therefore, dismissive of his influence on his writing. Schopenhauer's philosophy points to the unconscious; he refers to the inner contradiction manifested as desire. He also appears to provide the precursor to Lacanian notions of lack, suggesting all willing springs from lack. The constant longing and suffering leads Schopenhauer to propose "a return to the night of unconsciousness wherein is found the peace of the all-sufficient nothing", (Schopenhauer, cited in Dollimore, 2001, p. 173). Schopenhauer suggests we only accept death when we have overcome a powerful and irrational desire to live. Then death brings a wonderful release. The death wish, his model of instinctual drives, the "I", or the ego, as the dark point in consciousness, all suggest that Freud owes much to Schopenhauer. His work can be seen to have been a critical influence on Freud's work. He addresses loss, transience, and death almost a century before Freud.

> We do not become conscious of the three greatest blessings of life as such, namely health, youth and freedom, as long as we possess them, but only after we have lost them. Our real existence is only in the present, whose unimpeded flight into the past is a constant transition into death, a constant dying. (Schopenhauer, 1966[1819], I.311)

Freud is, initially, tentative in his presentation of the death drive, but he pursues the notion of binding and unbinding and re-examines the origins of psychic pain. In *Civilization and its Discontents* (1930a) Freud writes of dissolution, of dissolving life back to a pre-organic state, literally to "dissolve those units and to bring them back to their primaeval, inorganic state. That is to say, as well as Eros there was an instinct of death" (Freud, 1930a, p. 118). Freud continues to offer dissolution as a key part of this topography, but his presentation of the death drive in *Civilization and its Discontents* also presents the more aggressive and sadistic elements of the death drive.

> men are not gentle creatures who want to be loved, and who at the most can defend themselves if they are attacked; they are, on the contrary, creatures among whose instinctual endowment is to be reckoned a powerful share of aggressiveness. As a result, their neighbour is for them not only a potential helper or sexual object, but also someone who tempts them to satisfy their aggressiveness on him to exploit his capacity for work without compensation, to use him sexually without his consent, to seize his possessions, to humiliate him, to cause him pain, to torture and to kill him. Homo homini lupus. (Freud, 1930a, p. 111)

Freud describes human beings as constantly inclined towards aggression to one another, that there is a great struggle against self-destruction, that society is literally and perpetually threatened with disintegration. The struggle against self-destruction, a phenomenon much in evidence in psychology (Frosh, 2012), marries well with Freud's notion of a death drive. The death drive has not been embraced with the same passion as some of Freud's other theories: for example, Lear's (2000) fundamental critique that the death drive for Freud is an "enigmatic signifier" that lacks the depth of a properly worked through theory. The "nirvana principle", a subsidiary idea has gained some approval (Piven, 2004). In nirvana, one almost wills oneself into a state of unconsciousness and death, where struggles and pain can disappear. Freud's portrayal of the combat of Eros and Thanatos is of opposing powerful forces, locked in combat. Were his attention to have been focused on the subject of this research, he might well have reported that the struggle resulted in a triumphant death.

> And now, I think, the meaning of the evolution of civilization is no longer obscure to us. It must present the struggle between Eros and death, between the instinct of life and the instinct of destruction as it work itself out in the human species. This struggle is what all life essentially consists of, and the evolution of civilization may therefore be simply described as the struggle for life of the human species. (Freud, 1930a, p. 122)

As we noted earlier, Freud states that there is no death in the unconscious, yet he moves to make the death instinct central to his thinking. Freud's preoccupation with an internal force of dissolution captured in *Beyond the Pleasure Principle* (1920g) develops in *Civilization and its Discontents* (1930a) to a destructive force directed towards the world in general. In Freud's return to the death drive, this writing occurred at a time when the ravages of the First World War could be understood and that the violence and aggression of war was very much on the surface. The clash of desire and civilisation leads Freud to the notion that there is something impossible about the fulfilment of human desire. The incompatibility of libidinal instinct and complete satisfaction is something that Freud raised early on in *Totem and Taboo* (Freud, 1912–1913).

The death drive was characterised by a drive towards an inorganic state, a state of nothingness, or nirvana, and offers a contrast to his more willingly received life drive linked to sexual urges and desires for satisfaction. Cited as the most controversial of Freud's contributions (Akhtar, 2011), it caused considerable controversy. Libido and aggression here are on equal footing. Jones (1961), in his biography of Freud, acknowledges the limited objective support the drive theory received. Winnicott, too, has no place for death drive, yet there is a place for aggression acknowledged; in Winnicott's thinking, this is seen as being "synonymous with activity" (1975, p. 204). Freud's drive theory pits sexual urges against ego preservation urges and death drives against those committed to life (Frosh, 2012).

Loss vs. *desire*

As we have identified, it is love rather than loss that is commonly regarded as the obsession of psychoanalysis (Benjamin, 1988; Freud, 1915b; Lear, 1998). Freud is most customarily associated with desire, with the public acknowledgement of sexual drives, drives that are on the border of the psychic and the physical. His work brought sexuality to the fore at a time when cultural norms presented and limited sexuality to a reproductive function. First, in *The Interpretation of Dreams* (1900a) Freud stripped dreams of their disguises to reveal their erotic content, and depicted the constancy and repetition of our desires.

Freud's *Three Essays on the Theory of Sexuality* (1905d) distinguished sexuality as a drive, or a set of component drives. He introduced the concept of the libido, the means to generate erotic attachments, an energy with which mental processes and structures are invested. The identification of an infantile form of sexuality was a shocking contribution at the time. Freud's development of the Oedipus complex became a central tenet of psychoanalytic theory. Here, each individual struggles to possess the mother and destroy all rivals for her love and attention.

While central and of continuing validity to psychoanalytic theory, the Oedipus complex has death at its heart. The child is reared by two parents, mother and father. The infant's first and primal relationship is with the mother—she is at the heart of everything and the answer to all the infant's needs. The rupture of this intimate relationship is carried out by the father and he becomes the focus of the murderous impulses of the child. The relationship between mother and father excludes the child; therefore, the child will kill off the father and return to the intimate and all-encompassing bond with the mother. The Oedipus complex can also be "inverted", with the father the object of desire. In this scenario, the complex is much more masochistic and, even, death driven. The place of Oedipus at work has been explored (Schwartz, 1992; Stein, 2007) but the element of death in Oedipus, and death itself, has been given much less attention. The common emotion in the Oedipus complex is not love, but hate; the child is caught between the necessity of choosing between two objects. The child's emotional reaction to both is of hatred, hatred of the mother because she denies herself to him and hatred of the father as his rival (Simmel, 1944).

The domination of the pleasure principle

According to Freud, there are two principles that govern mental activity: the pleasure principle and the reality principle. For Freud, the pleasure principle is innate and does not need to be learnt, whereas the reality principle is learnt during development through interaction with the fact and objects of the external world (Rycroft, 1962). We see, therefore, that Freud presented his theory with a commitment to the dominance of the pleasure principle in mental life. Sexual impulses, according to psychoanalysis, are repressed and prevented from direct expression, so they appear when there is an opening, in dreams, in jokes, and in slips of the tongue. Equally forceful is the sexual repression that forces a lid on these impulses when they seek to emerge. Freud, here, offers us a remarkable insight: the complicity of impulse and repression. The foundation of psychoanalysis is rooted in love and desire. Ideas of libido, repression, desire, and infantile sexuality have become established as central tenets of psychoanalysis.

> In the theory of psycho-analysis we have no hesitation in assuming that the course taken by mental events is automatically regulated by the pleasure principle. We believe, that is to say, that the course of those events is invariably set in motion by an unpleasurable tension, and that it takes a direction such that its final outcome coincides with a lowering of that tension—that is, with an avoidance of unpleasure or a production of pleasure. (Freud, 1920g, p. 7)

The tendency of patients to repeat situations that caused them pain and their resistance to respond to therapeutic efforts that might alleviate symptoms led Freud to rethink his theories on drives and anxieties. The constant re-emergence of difficult and unpleasant emotions, for example, in dreams, led Freud to reconsider the aim of all drives to be the experience of pleasure. His work developed to propose a rethinking of the pleasure principle. The death drive was not presented in opposition to the life drive, but as a reconceptualisation of the order in which pleasure was sought; sexual drives, in this framework of thinking, become a secondary rather than a primary drive.

> Eros, the life drive, aims at combining whereas Thanatos, the death drive, aims at destroying. The drives are postulates with implications, not observables. Freud's immediate aim in postulating them was to open up a developmental stage of "binding" the two drives to that they fuse and so the possibility that they could be "bound" together in different ways with different results during development and that they could also unbind. (Tuckett, 2007, pp. 70–71)

There is a contradictory nature to Freud's writing on death. It is not something that appears in our unconscious, yet he urges us to engage with death. We think too much about death, we think too little about death. We are obsessed with death and we avoid death (1915b).

Bion presents another dimension to the pleasure principle. His theory emerges from the fascination of what goes on in the consulting room and he describes the process by which a patient moves from evading pain towards acceptance of suffering, in opposition to the pleasure principle.

Summary

This chapter has provided an overview of death in psychoanalytic thought and introduced the theoretical foundation on which this research draws. Theoretical material was organised and presented around the subheadings of (i) the impossibility of death, (ii) working through death, (iii) nothingness *vs.* destruction, and (iv) loss *vs.* desire.

Key thinking from Freud and post Freudian thinkers, notably Klein and Bion, were covered. Attention was also given to existential philosophers in the field of psychology whose inclusion is relevant to a discussion of death and psychoanalysis. The way in which death has been explored and understood within psychoanalysis was presented.

These concepts are considered later in relation to organisational life and their relevance to corporate decay.

CHAPTER THREE

Death and organisations

Death and organisations have been examined from a number of perspectives: trying to understand the notion of mortality in an organisational context takes us from genocide to suicide at work, from the death of a leader to the closure of a department. It encompasses grief and loss at work and parting ceremonies.

This chapter is structured in three parts. First, death and grief in organisations is explored, looking at models of loss in the first instance and including traditional models of mourning, such as that of Kubler-Ross (1969). Grief and loss at work are then given attention, including the death of a leader in the workplace and the impact of mergers and downsizing on the process of loss. Second the chapter examines extreme expressions of death at work through the subject of genocide as a brutal and efficient execution of murder at work; showing how it requires organisational skills and expertise to execute such dirty work. The third and final part of the chapter tackles the way in which organisations defend themselves against death: for example, through denial and greed.

Together, these examinations of death and organisations provide an overview of the way in which death has been treated at work, placing the research in the context of current examinations of death at work.

Death and grief in organisations

The case has been made in the preceding chapter that we are experiencing a vulnerability of working life where, increasingly, organisational collapse is a feature of our everyday experience (Cederstrom & Fleming, 2012; Comfort, 2013; Samuel, 2010). Endings can be experienced as a profound source of loss and suffering (Cunningham, 1997; Driver, 2007, 2009; Harris & Sutton, 1986). The collapse of large financial institutions, corporate giants, and high street stores, as well as numerous small and medium sized enterprises, means that organisational death is a feature of working life in this early part of the twenty-first century.

Organisational death has received some attention, in terms of pathology, and investigation as to why the organisation has failed through a diagnostic model of failure encompassing the various disorders and illnesses that might affect the life chances of an organisation. The focus on the downfall and disappearance of organisations usefully highlights the tendency for organisational success to draw more attention and interest than organisational failure (Samuel, 2010). Organisational decline and death is receiving attention, for example, focusing on models for understanding organisational failure (Mellahi & Wilkinson, 2004). This book is a contribution to the debate, yet its concern is not why organisations fail. Its focus, as identified at the outset, is on the participants' experience of the collapse and the lessons to be learnt from that experience.

Loss and grief are part of everyday experience that is felt no less keenly in the workplace. These responses to loss are experienced in organisations when an organisation ceases to exist, or a department shuts down, or when a leader dies. In attempting to understand loss and grief, different frameworks and models have been developed; these topics are now given attention.

Models of loss

The consequence of loss was examined psychoanalytically in the previous chapter with an exploration of Freud's work, "Mourning and melancholia". This distinguished Freud's examination of normal and pathological responses to loss. Bowlby developed Freud's notion to develop attachment theory (1961). Bowlby's work on the pathological potential of loss was influenced by both Freud and Klein. His psycho-analytic training at the British Psychoanalytic Institute was conduc-ted at a time, in the 1930s, when Klein's influence was considerable and her mark on the developmental origins of his work is evident. Bowlby's paper on mourning, "Grief and mourning in infancy and early childhood" (1960), caught the attention of Parkes (1972), whose research area into adult bereavement was established. His study, involving a non-clinical group of widows, was known to influence Kubler-Ross (Parkes, 1972). Parkes and Bowlby collaborated and further developed the examination of adult grief to define four phases of grief: numbness, yearning and protest, disorganisation and despair, and reorganisation (Bowlby & Parkes, 1970).

Bowlby later developed this model of bereavement and construc-ted a phased model that included numbness, yearning, searching and anger, disorganisation and despair, and reorganisation (Bowlby, 1980). He saw these as sequential phases that are worked through. Parkes visited Kubler-Ross while she was gathering data for her influential 1969 book and the development of her work can be seen to have been influenced by both Parkes and Bowlby.

Kubler-Ross is perhaps the most commonly referred to creator of a model of grief. *On Death and Dying* (1969) was inspired by her work with terminally ill patients. Her contribution was significant and led to changes in the care of the terminally ill in the USA and beyond. The influence of psychoanalytic theory on the development of this model is clear.

Kubler-Ross presents a five-stage model of grief that a person and/or their survivors will experience when confronted with impend-ing death. This hypothesis offers stages of denial, anger, bargaining, depression, and acceptance; these might be experienced in no par-ticular order and not necessarily all stages will be experienced as each loss will be unique. Kubler-Ross also tackles the issue of resis-tance to the subject of death and describes the struggle of hospital staff to engage with the subject of death and dying. She notes that those with experience of loss employed fewer defence mechanisms and were more readily able to face death as a reality. She also distinguishes between doctors and nurses and identifies nurses as being more com-fortable engaging with the topic. She cites Cicely Saunders, founder of the modern hospice movement, a nurse first, then medical social worker, and then physician, as expert at dealing with matters of death with comfort: ". . . since she does not need denial she is unlikely to meet much denial in her patients" (Kubler-Ross, 1969, p. 248).

Kubler-Ross describes how she guides medical staff through fright, helplessness, and feelings of impotence towards a more familiar and accepting attitude towards death. Some application of her work has been made to organisational life in the field of organisational change (Elrod & Tippett, 2002; Zell, 2003).

Zell draws parallels with Kubler-Ross's stages of death and dying in a study of a large public university to explain individual and group level responses to change. Using data gathered as part of a change management programme, Zell (2003) identified that professors in the physics department responded to change in ways that resembled the stages of death and dying identified by Kubler-Ross. Zell reports that, like the terminally ill, the faculty went through periods of denial, anger, bargaining, depression, and, ultimately, acceptance.

Elrod and Tippett (2002) use bereavement theory as part of their review of the human response to change and transition, of which loss and death is central. They title their paper "The 'death valley' of change" and credit Kubler-Ross as one of the first writers to succinctly develop a stage process to understanding change. However, they prioritise Lewin's stage model of change as most influential, incorporating the three phases of unfreezing, moving, and freezing (1952). They identify as most challenging the intermediary stage, in both the Lewin and the Kubler-Ross models, resulting in a reduction in capabilities.

The Kubler-Ross model of grief has been applied widely and extended beyond responses to individual experiences of death. Some, however, question Kubler-Ross as offering a universally applicable model of dying and resist the categorisation of the mourning experience (Douglas, 2004; Terry, 2012). There is also resistance to the holistic description of the mourning process, one that has a beginning and an end, the question is raised as to what propels individuals through the stages and prevents them from being stuck in an endless loop of grief (Archer, 1999; Zell, 2003). Zell does not refer to melancholia, but melancholia is akin to what she describes as the "stuckness" in grief.

Blau (2006) proposed a model to understand victim responses to organisation closure that builds on Kubler-Ross's work. This work was followed by a further study (Blau, 2007) where grieving stages were measured and clustered into "grieving categories". These were negative, incorporating denial, anger, bargaining, and depression, and positive, incorporating exploration and acceptance. Temporal issues, as well as a measure of which grieving stage had the biggest impact, were considered and greater anger was found to be the most influential negative factor, leading to greater incivility, higher strain, and deviance. Acceptance was found to be the most influential grieving stage, leading to lower strain and lower incivility and deviance. In applying these modelling techniques to Kubler-Ross's stages of grief and mourning, Blau characterises destructive grieving (denial, anger, bargaining, and depression) and constructive grieving (exploration and acceptance) in a neat synthesis and furthers his argument with the strain imposed on those stuck in the destructive grieving process (Blau, 2007). His two-year study of a site closure applies this model (Blau, 2008).

Ritual processes associated with organisational closure have been highlighted by Harris and Sutton (1986). Ritual acts, such as parting ceremonies, are explained as important in allowing employees to separate from the organisation and the demands associated with organisational death. Sutton (1987) develops this thinking, drawing attention to the social aspect of members and previous members coming together to bid the organisation farewell. A model of understanding organisation endings is considered at the University of Gothenburg, Sweden, where the type of organisational ending is being linked to the type of end of life decisions and options chosen: for example, palliative care with an accepted care plan, assisted death with a joint decision to end life, or even ritual killing, where the end might be perceived as a gift to others (Arman, 2014).

The life cycle model of organisations is supported by a number of proponents (Galbraith, 1982; Whetten, 1987) who see organisations evolve in a variety of different stages. These scholars do not necessarily agree on what those stages might be, yet do concur that organisations move through a cycle of birth, growth, maturity, ageing, and death. This is seen as akin to the biological life cycle (Daft, 2004). Organisational pathology is given further attention by Samuel (2010), who applies the biological metaphor of a sick organisation.

> Deficiencies and malfunctions, which endanger the strength and survival of organizations, are treated here as pathologies. Organizational crime, corruption, and other related phenomena are similarly

dealt with in this context, as representing abnormalities that threaten the existence of organizations. (Samuel, 2010, p. 2)

Closedown, or organisational death (Sutton, 1987), has also invoked the biological metaphor. Sutton explores the transition to death through research designed to develop a model that could be translated to other organisational deaths. His work concentrated on unambiguous organisational death, that is, organisations that were defunct and their function or task no longer in operation (Sutton, 1987). In writing about the process of organisational death, Sutton treats biological death and organisational death as one and the same. Yet, when a biological system dies, so do all of its components, with the exception of organ transplantation, and this is not true for organisations with human members. Sutton argues terms such as closing or termination do not sufficiently or satisfactorily convey the loss of an organisation to displaced members; it is perhaps more similar to the loss of a friend or relative (Harris & Sutton, 1986).

Hasanen (2010) points out that in biological death, all components of the system die, whereas in organisational death, the human component lives on. The contrast between failure and death is brought out by Samuel (2010). He notes that while failure is reversible, for example, in a turnaround or management buyout situations, death is not reversible.

These models provide different frameworks in which to examine loss and mourning. The chapter now turns to grieving workers, the destructiveness of organisations, and the loss of a leader and departing employees.

Loss in the workplace

In the previous chapter, the notion of the "perennial mourner" (Volkan, 2007) was discussed, where the absent person is kept perpetually alive through mental representation and linking objects. Such mourners do not necessarily develop a depression, but almost freeze the mourning process and "introject" the lost person. The impact of grieving workers on organisational wellbeing is explored through institutional responses to grieving employees, largely from the perspective of the employee's loss of a loved one (Hazen, 2008). She presents an analysis of the economic cost of grieving employees. In cases of shared trauma,

Hazen identifies work as part of the healing process; for example, the Cantor Fitzgerald survivors of 9/11 (Barbash, 2006).

The concept of mourning applied to those experiencing the loss of work and organisation is also tackled by Gabriel (2012). Organisational mortality presents an opportunity for examination of systemic and individual loss. Gabriel offers psychoanalytic insights into dramatic organisational change, applying a theory of organisational miasma. The infected and contagious pollution of miasma powerfully evokes the drama of organisational life going through change, closure, and reinvention. The below-the-surface descriptions capture the essence of working within the brutal environment of a corporate rebrand and reinvention. Gabriel recognises the place for melancholia during corporate chaos and loss, yet his examinations of unfinished and unexplored mourning create this dark environment, the miasma, absent in the work of this research. Collective grief in work organisations is also given some attention in the case of major organisational change (Zell, 2003) or plant closure (Harris & Sutton, 1986).

Zell describes organisational change as a process of death, dying, and rebirth. Using the study of a university department of physics (as described earlier in relation to Kubler-Ross), she also draws on psychoanalytic theory to support her argument, citing "Mourning and melancholia" (Freud, 1917e) in an argument that supports this thesis. She acknowledges, as this writing does, that the professionals of her study are not dying, but that part of them is dying and that this loss has to be mourned. "For the physicists, their object of love was multifaceted and included the past prestige and stature of their field, the freedom to pursue their research specialties, and to teach the courses they desired" (Zell, 2003, p. 79).

Harris and Sutton look at parting ceremonies in six closing organisations and develop a theory that the parties and celebrations associated with the closure are a way in which the managers can influence the course of the organisation's demise and a way to help members cope with the closure. The following invitation to a wake for a dying organisation illustrates management efforts.

> The wake is to be an occasion to remember the vigor and charm of the departing spirit. We are interested in recalling and sharing memories of the place with those who were its friends and who may have benefitted from their association with it over the years. If you cannot

attend, please consider sending a message perhaps containing an
anecdote you remember with pleasure. (Harris & Sutton, 1986, p. 5)

Parting ceremonies, be they picnics, parties, or social gatherings, were
dominant in six of the eight closures studied, and "appear to be preva-
lent in organizational death" (Harris & Sutton, 1986, p. 6). Closure is
emotionally charged; it involves the loss of a social arena and of relationships. These ceremonies serve a function for the displaced member: "the members are at once providers and receivers of support and
coping strategies" (Harris & Sutton, 1986, p. 11). Despite the range
of celebrations evidenced (wake, lunch, big party, picnic), all shared
common elements, such as the expression of both sadness and anger,
the consumption of food and alcohol, the sharing of stories, and
the taking of photographs. These common themes, argue Harris
and Sutton, are in response to the demands placed on its members
of organisational death and a way of bringing some control to the
situation.

The emotional response to organisational death is examined by
Cunningham (1997). The participant observation study assumes that
those affected by an organisation's death, its members, but also clients
and associated organisations, experience similar feelings as when a
person dies. The paper opens with two examples of displaced individuals who are affected by organisational death and, in their inability to
cope, seek refuge in their organisation's generous disability programme. Cunningham's premise is that closure is a traumatic experience and some are better equipped than others to cope with disconnection and reconnection to another role. He argues, through his
long-term study of a dying community club, that the trauma of the
disconnection encourages a dependence on leaders and that those
who take longest to accept the inevitability of the end were those
unwilling to express their feelings and concerns.

Death of a leader

As we project on our leaders the templates of close childhood bonds,
the loss of a leader at work can resonate and distress those working in
an environment where the leader dies or is unexpectedly removed.
"Leaders awaken in their follower' fantasies and desires first experienced in childhood in those early relations with parents, which act as

templates for our subsequent encounters with authority and power" (Gabriel, 1999, p. 165).

The death of a leader is unusual and can tell us about the reactions to loss more generally within organisations. The importance of studying the impact of a leader's death was investigated through the empirical study of the sudden death of a health service leader (Hyde & Thomas, 2003). The study investigates the death of a community mental health team leader. The authors begin by describing reactions to loss through the Freudian notion of mourning and the defensive responses of denial or repression. Hyde and Thomas draw parallels with the loss of a leader at work and the loss of a family member or close relation. It is acknowledged that very often work relationships are more frequently and more easily broken than those relationships between family members (Hirschhorn & Gilmore, 1989). Health services often work on strongly hierarchical grounds that create a convergence on a leader and staff can become prone to dependency while idealising the leader (Kets De Vries, 1989).

Loss of a colleague as a result of moving to another job can also generate painful emotions that are stressful. An unconscious response to the stress and anxiety of the departure might be denial. Colleagues might well continue to behave as if the individual were never leaving. Moylan (1994) cites the example of a consultation where such an observation was required to help staff face up to the reality and loss of their highly valued colleague leaving and the individual to face up to the fact that their new opportunity also created loss—of relationships and a job that was enjoyed.

Catastrophic anxiety at the thought of loss and ending can lead to anger and attack (Salzberger-Wittenberg, 2013). It is painful to part and that parting is made more manageable by providing a space to address and face that ending. This issue was addressed for trainees at the Tavistock Clinic by the introduction of an annual instituted ending event, where feelings about endings could be shared (Salzberger-Wittenberg, 2013). Members of staff can also experience difficulties in adjusting to a new leader, particularly in the case of a dominant or charismatic leader. The loss of a controlling leader, committed to the team and generating great loyalty and involvement in her dying days led to staff struggles; staff had become used to depending on their previous leader to make decisions and they struggled to cope with their independence (Hyde & Thomas, 2003). In an anxious time, fears of persecution could be projected on others in order to retain the safety of the group (Hinshelwood & Skogstad, 2000).

Replacement of a leader is, therefore, a loss keenly felt and an attachment not easily replaced, despite the logic or merits of such a replacement. In the case of Hyde and Thomas's health service study, the leader had died and, therefore, replacement by another individual was inevitable. We turn to Freud to explain this reluctance to give up on a loss, the reality of the demand to forego any attachment to the object that no longer exists. "This demand arouses understandable opposition—it is a matter of general observation that people never willingly abandon a libidinal position, not even, indeed, when a substitute is already beckoning to them" (Freud, 1917e, p. 244).

Such loss can fuel fantasies for those who remain and evoke conflicting emotions of release or rejection; renegotiation of work practices will need to be established with the newly appointed leader and, finally, fantasies held about the leader as omnipotent will be affected (Hyde & Thomas, 2003). In a slow closedown situation, that loss is repeated again and again. The organisation faces ultimate demise but, in the run up to that date of closure, multiple losses occur, with colleagues taking redundancy, finding new jobs, or moving on in other ways. Employees might also experience a sense of manic triumph (Speck, 1994) in that they have survived while others have not.

Stokes (1994) describes the role consultancy process conducted by a nurse who had organised bereavement training for nurses, only to reveal her own intention to leave the department, offering a "bereavement" which could be discussed and learnt from. Bereavement can, therefore, be experienced at work through the loss of a leader but also through the departure of a member of staff.

Mergers and downsizing

Downsizing can be a series of endings for those experiencing a rationalisation process. Describing the closure of a department or ending of an organisational function as downsizing is a euphemism used as a means to sanitise the impact of organisational death on its members, in a sense to avoid the potential pain of the loss of those affected (Stein, 1998). The paring down of function or role can lead to a division in responsibility that brings with it survivors and victims. Loss of trust and additional stress in a downsizing operation can be experienced as grief. Kets de Vries and Balazs (1997) explore the impact of downsizing on the inner world of the stakeholders affected.

Their study looks at the roles of different players in the downsizing process, such as victims and survivors, and pays special attention to the role of "executioner", the senior employees with the responsibility to implement the downsizing process. This links to Arman's identification of murder in organisational death (2014). These individuals often have to abandon their personal values and belief system, the very values that led them to senior roles, in order to execute the downsizing plans. They do this by becoming detached and focusing on the organisational targets. However, such efforts lead to further stress, with reactions among staff including depression, substance abuse, hostility, and absenteeism (Leana & Feldman, 1988; Noer, 1993; Smith, 1994). Those responsible for the removal of employees adopted defensive patterns such as isolation, aggression, self-aggrandisement, scapegoating of the victims, dissociation, and depression. By looking at the psychological effects of those conducting the downsizing, Kets de Vries and Balazs offer a way of reframing downsizing to make it a less destructive process. This study provides a good example of the way in which the experience of organisational loss can be understood psychoanalytically from the viewpoint of a number of differing stakeholders.

Writing from the perspective of bankruptcy, Sheppard (1994) offers a definition of organisational death that relates to the function it no longer performs. It does not demand closure or decline but a change of focus or service. "The most straightforward way to define organizational death is to simply say that the organization dies when it stops performing those functions we would expect from it" (Sheppard, 1994, p. 796).

This definition is limited, as it lacks clarity around those organisations whose functions change or which streamline and continue to operate. Reversing the biological metaphor, it seems to suggest that a human being with some kind of disability is no longer alive. An organisation closedown might not happen in isolation. A business could be subsumed or be taken over. Loss of control in a buy-out or a merger is considered to be a death by some (De Gooijer, 2009). "When two organizations combine, at least one ceases to exist and this must be considered a death. If a merger involves a dominant partner, then the subordinate organization dies" (Carroll & Delacroix, 1982, p. 180).

There is also interest in organisational death in a preventative manner, that is, examination of the criteria that might lead to a lessening of the incidence of failure and decline. Findings such as the positive impact of interorganisational links and the negative impact of a firm's financial leverage also cite early turnaround efforts to counteract organisational inertia (Sheppard, 1994).

Organisational ecologists see dissolution as a sign of failure, determined by four factors: population density, industry life cycle, organisation age, and organisation size (Mellahi & Wilkinson, 2004). An ecological approach to organisational endings perceives them to be functioning as part of a natural system. In this paradigm, organisations respond to the environmental conditions they are situated in as live organisms. Organisations share a common interest in the survival of that system and work together to protect that system (Scott, 1992). Others view organisational closure as political process (Hardy, 1985).

Closedown or closure has been adopted in some management literature to alleviate the confusion of other restructuring or change efforts (Bergman & Wigblad, 1999; Hansson & Wigblad, 2006). Kelly and Riach's 2012 study in the UK financial services sector challenges this with a mythical analysis invoking Frankenstein as a metaphor for reanimating the dying organisation. Persistent failure manifests itself in organisational damage to itself and to stakeholders; these organisations may "bleed" and, ultimately, face their demise. Addressing the phenomenon of persistent failure, Meyer and Zucker (1989) offer a theory that is temporal and examines efficiency. Such treatment would most typically be applied to public bodies.

De Gooijer (2009) examines the shadow side of mergers. In *The Murder in Merger*, she examines the organisational psychodynamic of persecution and annihilation in mergers. Her work captures the human cost of dramatic organisation change. Fundamental to her analysis is the organisation-in-the-mind (Armstrong, 2005). Organisations are systems of meaning and objects held internally by employees. This close bond with the organisation, this unconscious image, means that the ending of part or all of an organisation is experienced as a symbolic destruction (De Gooijer, 2009, p. 175). She postulates that the organisation, before it is reformed in merger, goes through a destruction experienced as no less than catastrophic by the employees. Such catastrophe evokes defence mechanisms of splitting and denial, distancing employees emotionally from the organisation. Using Klein

(1975) to illustrate how different parts of the organisation were split into good and bad, she shows how employees projected brutality into managers who, in turn, projected their own destructive tendencies on employees.

Leaders and managers were seen as persecutory, cruel, and heartless. However, later in the study some evidence emerged of reparation and an understanding of management as a good object that could behave destructively. De Gooijer highlights the lack of space and opportunity for mindful thinking about huge change and potential destruction. The absence of this space to deal with possible annihilation is a central point made by the study. Yet, a merger, by its nature, is redefining boundaries that inherently evoke fear. In such cases, boundaries can be experienced as persecutory and be their own source of anxiety (Hirschhorn, 1988). The highly charged emotional arena of a merger involves the symbolic killing off of certain parts of an organisation. Organisational death involves a cessation of that entity; the function and space it occupies no longer exists.

Genocide: organised death

Bringing about large-scale death in a methodical and efficient manner requires organisational skills and expertise. Studies on genocide might not seem like an appropriate vehicle to examine endings in organisations, yet there are a number of insights that can be derived from this. Engaging with genocide as a phenomenon is worthwhile; organisational processes that make genocide possible should be considered and the applicability with which these processes apply to non-genocidal situations. Any genocide will involve complex activities, well thought out and executed. Issues of power and authority, decision-making, delegation, processes, and procedures will apply. In this respect, the link to organisational death is relevant and appropriate.

Genocide and organisations

Within genocide are the ingredients to operate any large-scale organisation: for example, co-operation between different parties, logistics, intelligence, and networking. Stokes and Gabriel (2010) argue that it is wrong to cite genocide as exceptional and, while cautious and respectful of the suffering and pain of victims of any holocaust, they draw compelling parallels, such as between ethnic cleansing and symbolic cleansing in organisations and between genocide and downsizing. The authors argue that there are lessons to be learnt from genocide for humankind and for various academic disciplines, including organisational theory.

The application of genocide to our understanding of organisations has also been tackled by Stein (2009). In "Death imagery and the experience of organizational downsizing, or is your name on Schindler's list?", Stein examines the contrast between the promises of productivity, quality, and profit improvements as a result of downsizing and the devastating impact of such restructuring. This change is seen as a form of sacrifice that buys organisational life through symbolic death. He uses the metaphor of the Holocaust to separate bad from good and as a means to secure rebirth through the expulsion of death. Lyotard (1993) relates suffering on its own scale; for example, a child bullied in the playground will, in his or her own mind, experience this as a crime against humanity.

The danger of engaging in a sensitive subject with the possibility of offence or awkward arguments is important: "the disciplines of management and organizational studies cannot remain passive audiences of these struggles" (Stokes & Gabriel, 2010, p. 17).

Stokes and Gabriel (2010) also raise the issue of morality in relation to genocide probing and question the subject of genocide as a failure in morality or a case of excessive application of a moral position. An exaggerated zeal in adopting the other position—the right against the wrong, the powerful against the weak or the entitled against the undeserving—becomes an essential feature. However, they give this death instinct energy and force that was never intended by Freud. In fact, Freud rejects any notion of the death drive having energy; he calls it the *destrudo* in contrast to the *libido*, to make this point.

Milgram's (1974) experiment into how humans can be coerced into performing unpleasant and abhorrent actions is relevant to discussions of the Holocaust and beyond. Involvement in genocide raises moral questions that may equally be raised in cases of mass redundancies associated with closure (Stein, 2001; Uchitelle, 2006). The question of why ordinary people in organisations do morally questionable or bad things when asked is at the heart of the debate on power and ethics. Organisations have an overpowering effect on the controlling members and the controlled (Clegg et al., 2007).

Bauman's (1989) contribution to the debate in *Modernity and the Holocaust* has been influential in taking the experience of the Holocaust beyond that of the victims of that genocide and the ubiquity of destruction. Bauman combines the psychosocial and the dirty work of the Holocaust to show that the Holocaust contained all the hidden possibilities of modern society, such as slavery and mass production. The application of scientific and rational organisation to mass extermination is presented here as a natural outcome of modernity. Alongside Bauman, Arendt's work in *Eichmann in Jerusalem* (1963) presents genocidal actions perceived by the perpetrators as normal and routine, hence the banality of evil. The price that needs to be paid for efficiency might be human life in the case of genocide; in the case of a shutdown or organisational closure, that can equate to a dehumanisation that allows the ending of livelihoods and career hopes. Bauer (2001) challenges Bauman, arguing that Nazi bureaucracy was not as efficient as portrayed and that brute force overcame such inefficiencies. Scholars also argue that both Arendt's and Bauman's theses ignore resistance and treat victims as passive. It has also been argued that both Arendt and Bauman ignore the ideology of German society (Allen, 2005, 2008; Bauer, 2001).

Allen further pursues the critique, arguing that, far from being mechanical, the Nazi genocide involved many committed, intelligent, and enthusiastic managers and professionals. Architects, chemists, and engineers worked individually and collaboratively to problem solve and innovate in a culture that valued these qualities. Indeed, Allen refers to this as the "business of genocide" (2002). There are also corporate collusions with genocide in the production of machinery, administrative systems, and provision of goods and services. In bringing notions of culture to discussions of the Holocaust, Allen is unusual in bringing current insights from organisational studies into the investigation of the Nazi Holocaust.

The triumph of genocide

The perpetrator and the victim, the clean and the unclean, the worthy and the unworthy, the powerful and the weak—all these polarisations are employed in a situation of genocide. Casting the other is fundamental to the "success" of genocide. Such positioning has parallels with organisational survival; the successful and the damned, the innovative and the old fashioned, the money-makers and the loss makers, the organisations with a future and the organisations without a future.

Positioning a group, individual, or object in contrast to oneself goes beyond scapegoating and allows identity to be formed in contrast to the notion of Other (Lacan, 1988). The Other is threatening and summons the separation of self from the authentic to the inauthentic. The Other is defined as inauthentic and, therefore, can be separated from the authentic self; in this way, it is possible to degrade, marginalise, and eradicate that which is inauthentic. These parts can be cast of and treated as "abjects" (Kristeva, 1982).

Freud (1921c, 1930a) termed aggression towards groups or individuals who are most like ourselves as narcissism of minor differences. Blok (2001), an anthropologist, applies this thinking to his work with the Mafia, where acts of violence are perpetrated against people who have been peaceful neighbours for years or even centuries. Recent examples illustrate this, for example, perpetrators and victims were often on friendly terms in the ethnic cleansing in Bosnia and the genocide of the Tutsis in Rwanda.

Ultimately, genocide is a subject worthy of respectful engagement with many psychological, social, political, and organisational processes that parallel organisational life. The sensitivity of suggesting any parallel between a job lay off or the closure of an organisation and the Holocaust and its atrocities and attendant loss of life and humanity prevents engagement with a subject that can teach us much about organisation, leadership, management, persecution, responsibility, communication, and professionalism.

Defences against death

The ego is protected through the function of defence and these defences may be activated by realistic dangers and threats. They are also activated by anxieties and tensions and threats to the superego. It is worth noting that anxiety is seen as a spur to development in psychoanalysis and, therefore, defences can be seen to play a part in normal development.

The conflict between the id (primal and hedonistic) and the super-ego (high-minded and performing the role of our consciences) is managed through the medium of the ego. It is through the application of defence mechanisms that individuals are able to hold on to their concept of self, literally to hold on to one's self. On occasions, the extensive application of defence mechanisms can be counterproductive and damaging, for example, preventing the formation of meaningful relationships, but, at other times, it protects the self intuitively from perceived threats. A defence mechanism differs from any thought-through coping strategies, as promoted through cognitive–behavioural therapy for example, as they are applied unconsciously and rooted in that which is hidden from ourselves.

Ego defence mechanisms can be activated by a tangible fear or threat, a need to suppress the primal id, or by some moral anxiety. Defence mechanisms allow the individual to manage and resolve their response to these fears. Defences against the disturbing and distressing thoughts surrounding organisational ending are now considered.

The destructiveness of organisations and prevention of mourning

Anxieties of persecution and annihilation exist within organisations and defences against such fear leads to an inhibited capacity to think. By extension, such defences take up so much space that they also prevent the experience of love, mourning, or reparation.

> To the extent that the psychotic part of an organization predominates over the non-psychotic part, the predominate thinking (and behavior) defends against perceived threat and persecution from systems in the external world that the organization itself wishes to dominate, control or even annihilate. (Sievers, 2003, pp. 190–191)

The psychotic dynamics of the pension fund system (Sievers, 2003) provide an illustration of this hypothesis. People work hard towards an affluent retirement, building capital and financial security, and, in so doing, delude themselves that the more money that is accumulated the more certain it is that death can be kept in abeyance. Somehow, human mortality can be ignored through acquisition, attention to the

markets, and pursuit of greater wealth and riches. The inherent destructiveness of an organisation can be hidden behind a mask of health
(Hinshelwood, 1991). Sievers argues that this dynamic is extended to
those who work in the organisations that manage the funds of the
wealthy; he proposes that anxieties are channelled and shifted
through the financial system. He cites George Orwell's (1936) assertion
that money holds the place that God once held in society, giving it
profound importance and elevating it into a kind of religion. The
reduced certainty in "eternal life", a life after death in heaven, means
that the retirement phase is the last stage of life.

Sievers is curious that, despite the intrinsic link of mortality to the
literature on pension funds, beyond the statistical entity of mortality,
it is a subject left alone in the main. The confidence in the ever-increas-
ing growth of the pension fund market is akin to the confidence and
certainty that those who invest will live long lives and enjoy the fruits
of their successful investments. The blind spot is mirrored—death
might come early, funds might fail.

> As the capacity and need to discriminate between creativity and
> destructivity—the forces of life and death—become obsolete in an
> economy exclusively driven by abstract and commoditized money,
> the actual injuries, annihilations and deaths resulting from this econ-
> omy are not perceived and thus cannot be acknowledged. (Sievers,
> 2003, p. 202)

Pensions are designed to carry people through their final life
phase; Sievers suggests that it carries with it much more than the
financial comfort of retirement, but has been elevated to a commodi-
tised immortality. With that comes an inability to mourn or regret.

Freud hints at his own capacity for avarice. In correspondence
with Fliess (1899), he reported his worries about his own income and
financial situation: "My mood also depends very strongly on my earn-
ings. Money is laughing gas to me."

The closedown effect

More literature on organisational theory is based on an assumption of
growth than on an assumption of decline (Samuel, 2010; Hansson,

2004; Whetten, 1980). Hansson observes that declining organisations remain a neglected area. The challenge and difficulty of researching organisational closedowns is identified, due to the difficulty of accessing information . . . and the fact that the organizations often literally vanish (Hansson & Wigblad, 2006, p. 940).

Productivity increases associated with closedown has been labelled the "closedown effect". Hansson and Wigblad (2006) propose that this effect can be anticipated as a consequence of a closedown decision. Such pyrrhic victories for workers is examined for socially responsible and non-socially responsibly driven closures and found to be applicable to the latter as well as the former. A focus on the motivational aspects of closedown was also the subject of Hasanen's 2010 doctoral thesis (Stockholm University). This thesis builds on the work investigating the threat of closure of plant organisations and the subsequent increase in productivity (Hansson & Wigblad, 2006) and presents interesting data on the psychological impact of closedown.

Other studies have concentrated on the reasons for decline and failure of organisations, including Sheppard's investigation of bankruptcy (1994). Sutton (1987) carried out research to develop a process for dying organisations and identified continued and increased efforts by employees after the announcement of organisational death. Not all research has identified productivity improvements. Organisation downfall through merger (De Gooijer, 2009; Sher, 2013) focuses on the anxiety created in merging two organisations, threats and anxieties that are felt equally in a situation of organisational death.

Denial

"Chronic niceness" is a term that has been used to describe staff working in hospices whose dedication and care for the dying is a daily task (Speck, 1994). In such cases, any negative aspects of caring for the dying are split off and denied—this is something that the individual and the organisation collude in constructing, leading to a fantasy that all death is "nice". As dealing with death will inevitably stir up primitive, powerful, and unpleasant feelings from time to time, the death of a child or a tragic accident, for example, one must question where these negatives feelings go. In the case of an organisation such as a hospice, these feelings can be redirected into the management; "they are inefficient", "they do not understand", "they are demanding", etc. In splitting off the negative feelings of the work from themselves and their patients, these feelings of the staff are displaced into the management. There might also be similar feelings directed to family members seen as hypercritical or demanding. This is an indication that the staff group might have moved to what Klein would describe as paranoid–schizoid thinking to maintain work cohesiveness (Klein, 1959). Klein's idea of individual mania is brought to light in the context of the financial crisis by Stein (2011).

This work did much to highlight denial, omnipotence, triumphalism, and over-activity as typifying a manic culture.

> Applying this to the level of culture, a manic culture is one in which leaders and members observe and note problems and vulnerabilities, but feel threatened by their observations because they imply the need to worry and register the warning involved. Such a culture is therefore unable to use these observations in a healthy way and take the warning seriously. (Stein, 2011, p. 176)

Blindness to organisational collapse and disaster was given attention in another financial institution, a hedge fund that collapsed at the end of the 1990s (Stein, 2003). Here, Stein explores the possible explanation for the collapse of a highly invested, potent, and highly resourced and staffed hedge fund. He examines how the mighty fall as a result of unbounded irrationality and uses organisational narcissism to explain the lack of capacity to engage with the possibility of failure. Disasters rarely emerge out of the blue, and involve a period of incubation (Turner, 1978; Turner & Pidgeon, 1997). During this time, there is information there to indicate the impending collapse but this information is ignored.

Greed

Desire and greed for transformation is seen by Spielrein (1994[1912]) as a means of preservation, and the introjected objects as a means to protect the ego-ideal from an ever changing superego. Extending the idea of an ego-ideal to an organisation-ideal (Carr & Lapp, 2006; Marcuse, 1955), an organisation defending itself against anxieties of persecution and annihilation might mobilise splitting and excessive forms of introjection and projection to protect itself (Lawrence, 2000; Sievers, 1999). Sievers applies the notion to capitalist greed, looking at greed as inherent in capitalism and in financial crisis. Competition is viewed as fuelled by excessive greed, the desire to annihilate competitors, and a source of corruption and fraud (Sievers, 2012).

Driver (2008) looks at food in organisations with a discursive examination of thirty-five narratives. Seven of her thirty-five stories describe food as omnipresent. For some organisations in her study, food was integral to day-to-day routine. Food was used as a means of improving meetings, making training more appealing, or as a thank you. Driver points to the ubiquity of food at work and the importance of food practices to organisations (2008). However, what it represents to the employees can be interpreted differently. Food was a constant presence at Interbank, a daily display.

The Enron scandal of 2001 was a precursor of the banking crisis of 2008. While Enron was not a bank, it functioned very much on the same lines as an investment bank. Enron traded energy but acted like an investment bank, except an investment bank that was not regulated. Greed prevailed and the fraudulent practice was eventually uncovered by a whistle-blower. In this collapse and the later financial crisis, firms were motivated to behave inappropriately, and rewarded lavishly for doing so.

The 2004 scandal of the Parmalat Corporation, put into insolvency, yet saved by the government, provides a good example of personal generosity and philanthropy coupled with tremendous greed and deception (Long, 2008). Long highlights that the CEO's greed was allowed to flourish, and a blind eye was turned by colleagues and even auditors of the firm's practice. The climate of acquisition and success blinded the international bankers, lawyers, and accountants, preventing them from making sensible decisions.

Greed is treated as perverse by Long (2008), and by Levine (2005, p. 725) as the "ultimate narcissistic fulfilment". In a paper on the corrupt organisation, Levine (2005) questions whether corporate greed exists or whether this is actually a new kind of morality. He refers to Enron and the way in which securities analysts hailed the organisation as the very best of the best, unbeatable, yet, three years later, the organisation was in bankruptcy. The notion of Enron as a greedy corporation is unpicked further, Levine suggests that the executives prided themselves on creating a new, innovative, and revolutionary way of working—even, as Skilling, the Chief Operation Officer, described it, doing "God's work" (Levine, 2005, p. 726).

Organisational death as a cultural phenomenon

Bell and Taylor (2011) refer to the term "organisational death" as a means to describe events including downsizing, site closure, and business failure. Their work moves beyond a traditional examination of bereavement and explores the notion of continuing bonds. They offer this perspective as a means of supporting an understanding of organisational death as a cultural phenomenon. A greater understanding of organisations, and their meaning to their members, can be accessed through the collective experience of loss and grief (Bell & Taylor, 2011). Applying individual notions of bereavement to an understanding of loss and grief at a collective level is to be handled cautiously. Bell and Taylor look beyond models of letting go and moving on, popularised in psychological stage theories, and urge an engagement with organisational death as a valuable asset in constructing organisational meaning. They challenge the prevalence of linear and sequential stage models of loss and grief and argue that these models rest on assumptions they categorise as managerialist, cultural, and empirical. They argue persuasively for the value of common commitment and purpose in organisational death and that this should not be overlooked in pursuing tales of personal tragedy and vulnerability.

Death is the conclusion of life for most, but the continuation of scrutiny, invention, and analysis for the famous and powerful. RIP (Rest in Peace) is unlikely for those whose stories continue after their death and 2012 brought two striking examples: the canonisation of Steve Jobs of Apple (Bell & Taylor, 2012) and the demonisation of a previous "angel", Jimmy Savile (Mills et al., 2013). Their stories and lives will continue in the minds of the living long after their deaths. So, too, can an organisation continue to be part of national folklore and heritage after its demise—think of the mining industry, Enron, or British Steel. Death can also be a cue for idealisation and praise: the demise of Woolworths brought much nostalgia to the fore (yet, too little attention too late to save the business). Organisations can then have an existence beyond physical death, as can humans (Unruh, 1983; Walter, 2014).

Suicidology

The notion of symbolic death through alienation in the workplace (Cederstrom & Fleming, 2012) is now extended to the voluntary ending of physical life. The study of suicide has potential to provide an understanding of how people relate to work and to organisations. Often presented as individualistic, the study of suicide as an organisational issue is greatly under-researched and an organisational suicidology is proposed: "the study of suicide in the context of organization and organised work" (Cullen, 2014, p. 47). The reluctance to engage with the topic of death and face its inevitability (Kahn & Liefooghe, 2014; Kristeva, 2012) might explain why studies of death are so rare in organisational studies (Cullen, 2014).

Following a spate of employee suicides, some suggest as many as sixty, France Telecom made a public announcement stressing that the suicides were prompted by personal, not professional, reasons (Cederstrom & Fleming, 2012). However, despite the claims by senior executives at France Telecom that the suicide figures merely reflected the national suicide rate, the majority of suicides were linked to dissatisfaction with the restructuring of the firm. Since privatisation, 40,000 jobs had disappeared at France Telecom. The impact of the recession on suicide presents an increase in suicide rates among the unemployed and greater rises in suicide in those countries with the harshest financial crises, such as Greece and Ireland (Struckler et al., 2011). For Freud, suicide represented the killing off of the unwanted self (1912–1913).

There are several examples of suicides by troubled bankers, one jumping off the roof of a prestigious roof-top restaurant, champagne glass in hand, another throwing himself in front of a high-speed train, and a third by hanging in a five-star hotel. These big exits express "the preference for death over a non-life of work" (Cederstrom & Fleming, 2012, p. 59).

A miserable picture of workers half alive in an inauthentic engagement with the declared corporate values is portrayed in *Dead Man Working* (Cederstrom & Fleming, 2012). The corporate aim is clear: not only to make us do something we would rather shun, but also to make us want to do it (2012, p. 9). Hirschman's (1970) classic essay on organisational decline that cites exit, voice, or loyalty as potential responses to crisis in organisations is irrelevant when the individual becomes the corporation; there is no escape from yourself. Contemporary capitalism has been accused even of killing its worker's souls (Banerjee, 2008).

Such conditions create a climate where workers see death as preferable over life, and life as a fate worse than death. Death is seen as freedom, as expressed by a junior management consultant: "I realized things were bad whenever I boarded a plane for work, I always prayed it would crash". (Cederstrom & Fleming, 2012, p. 64). Freud's death instinct has potency in such expressions.

Summary

I began with an overview of the way in which death has been brought to work. The chapter examined grief and loss in the workplace, looking at different models and frameworks for examining organisational death. It emphasised the interest of this research in the experience of loss rather than the mechanics of organisational failure. Building on the theoretical foundations of Chapter Two, the relevance and importance of work and organisational death were highlighted.

The experience of grief and loss at work was examined. Models of loss and mourning were presented, such as Kubler-Ross's (1969) staged presentation of grief and Blau's (2006) study of organisational closure. Different ways of looking at death at work were examined, together with outcomes such as the closedown effect. A broad sweep of genocide, murder, and loss at work were then considered as well as the way in which an understanding of organisational processes can help to confront the subject of death at work. Subjects such as genocide and murder at work might seem extreme, but their relevance to understanding the mechanics of death at work was justified. The slippery and contradictory nature of death at work was considered. The frailty of life, where incidents and accidents can result in small wounds that heal quickly or life-ending events that involve a being's cessation, is troubling to bear.

In the financial world, such frailty is replicated. Mistakes or failed transactions can be easily recovered at times, but, at others, cause the ultimate downfall of an institution. Behaviour that had continued for years, inflicting hardly noticeable scratches on the corporate surface, at a certain time and in the eyes of certain bodies, can cause the ultimate death of that corporation.

DEATH AT WORK

Author's note:

In this part of the book, "Death at Work", the results of the research are presented.

Quotes from research interviews are indented and presented in quotation marks and observation notes are indented and presented in sans serif font.

CHAPTER FOUR

Mourning at work

"In mourning it is the world which has become poor and empty; in melancholia it is the ego itself"

(Freud, 1917e, p. 246)

The assumption that we have unconscious motivations that are not always understood by others, or, indeed, ourselves, is central to psychoanalysis. If, therefore, we accept that the self is divided, we accept there is an outside that has an impact on the inside; in other words, the psychosocial. This notion of internal and external worlds that struggle to communicate relates to the differences between mourning and melancholia. In mourning, there is recognition of the negative impact of loss and an understanding of the painful responses to that loss. This chapter deals with mourning in the organisation. In melancholia, that loss is harder to compute and, rather than being worked through, is trapped inside and becomes a self-persecuting internal object. The melancholic organisation is dealt with in Chapter Five.

The chapter presents the data gathered and interprets the experience of closure and loss within the framework of mourning. It offers an interpretation of loss through examples of experiences told and observed during the eighteen-month-long project. These results, and those in the following chapters, offer a theoretical contribution to understanding closure and acknowledging the painful experience of loss in both mourning and melancholia. In mourning, this loss is worked through, leading to an acknowledgement of the end.

Participants voiced their loss as something chaotic, disjointed, and multi-faceted. This polyphony of loss ranged from financial ruin to the betrayal of an idealised leader. Organisational death, as we have established, causes pain and suffering. Our work becomes part of ourselves, our identity, and the way in which we are defined (Parkes, 1972; Stapley, 1996). Organisation-in-the-mind (Armstrong, 2005) indicates how we internalise the organisations of which we are part and that attachment suggests the importance, continuity, and confirmation that organisation provides. When that reality is destroyed, employees must find some way to deal with their loss and change in circumstance.

The chapter presents a mourning organisation that works through the loss with recognition of an inevitable end; this is presented here via an acknowledgement of loss, recognition of the value of work, the way in which the anxiety of loss is contained, and the way in which the behaviour of the senior management is reconciled, leading to reparation.

Following Freud (1917), what characterises a mourning organisation from a melancholic organisation is the way in which that loss is processed. A mourning organisation takes an expected path of disappointment, but is able to integrate that loss as part of a broader experience of working life, and to move on. While there might be sorrow and distress, these symptoms do not convert into depression and despair. In the mourning organisation, the loss is worked through and integrated. Profound loss emerged strongly in the research data. For some, this loss was accepted with a stoic recognition that the good times could not have continued forever. Those individuals within the bank had benefited from the years of plenty and, therefore, had to shoulder the years of scarcity with dignity. This response resonates most closely with a healthy response to loss, like that of the mourner.

Working through

In psychoanalysis, working through is a technical term that refers to the piecemeal process by which the patient, in analysis, discovers the implication of an interpretation or insight. This fuller understanding is something that occurs over time. By extension, this can be applied to the process of getting over a loss or mourning. In mourning, there is a gradual acknowledgement that the lost object is no longer available where previously it had been a familiar figure (Rycroft, 1995).

Regular meetings, procedures, structure, tight management control of timekeeping, sick leave, and holiday habits were evident. The demise of the organisation did not result in a letting up of practice and procedures: on the contrary, at every management meeting I observed, team leaders were asked to update the meeting on the processes established and embedded. These measures can be seen as a means to contain the anxiety of the ending and as a mechanism to make the work bearable. The way in which the organisation worked through its loss is presented here in terms of acknowledgement of the end and reconciliation of the behaviour of senior management. In Kleinian terms, this was some kind of reparative process (Klein, 1984b[1940]).

Acknowledgement of the end

> "I think it's come to its natural end. Umm it's like a bereavement, not like a bereavement, or a mourning period, it's more that now, it's done now, but I'm, you know I learnt a lot at Interbank, I've taken a lot from it, its . . . I've met some fantastic people but that time is now the time to move on and do something different, you know, so it's not sad as such it's just, you know, it's time. So my time here I feel has come to an end."

An acknowledgement of the end of the organisation and the lifestyle and status it had afforded was expressed by some interviewees. This resignation was not necessarily the first response of interviewees, but a position that they had come to after recognising the fate of the institution and their own destiny outside its boundaries. There was reluctant acknowledgement by some that, as financial experts, they should have anticipated the impossibility of the continual rise of their fortune and their share portfolio. The following interviewee refers to the "true believer camp", a description of people who believed the hyperbole from the top of the bank about recovery, about this downturn in profit being a blip, and about a return to the good times; this was a hope that was clung to.

> "You would have probably belonged to the true believer camp, but all of a sudden realise that actually the numbers don't start to add up at this stage any more."

Another interviewee explains the way in which he profited from the success of the bank and his acknowledgement of the risk such practice entailed. He seems to be carrying out a posthumous review of his conduct and recognising that the good times were accepted without question; the bad times, therefore, should not be so surprising.

> "I recognise that I bought stocks and I bought shares. And you know what, there's a market and they go . . . I wasn't complaining when they were going up twenty per cent every year. I never once said no, actually stop, take it all back. I never once said that. So I don't think . . . I don't think it's pleasant having lost all of that but I understood the risk I took and the money, there it was on the table. I could have taken it off at any time I liked."

This response is most akin to a healthy response to loss that is presented in models of grief and mourning (Blau, 2006; Bowlby & Parkes, 1970; Kubler-Ross, 1969) and an illustration of the way in which the individuals concerned could separate their experience from themselves and move on. Some, then, were resigned to their financial loss, their investment grief, and the situation of the institution and wider economy. Those who joined Interbank knowing the end was in sight adopted a stance of using their time well, an expression of ability to be in the moment of the working world and maximise the opportunities on offer, such as training and development.

> "And you'll never get up the other side of the U curve when it comes to investment grief if you don't accept that, and if you can't forget it."

The place of the bank in the big picture of global economic melt-down was part of the acceptance expressed by some. The knowledge that Interbank's failure was just one of a series in the banking world offered some recognition and acceptance of the dire situation the organisation was in.

> "Christ! And we're fucked! That's it! The US banking industry is in trouble and this is just going to, like this is going to feed into the banking system of the world and every bank around the world."

In this way, the bank's downfall was integrated into the broader financial crisis, which led to a resignation of fortitude towards the collapse. There was still drama, shock, and horror. However, such acceptance can also be seen as a defence against the dismay of their personal circumstances. Pushing the collapse on to an external, world stage might help to defend victims of the collapse from the painful circumstance of their loss. Others expressed their financial loss in a more accepting way and with regard to their fortune in relation to others who had borrowed to gain further shares.

> "Everyone lost financially because of shares and all that kind of stuff. But if you put that to one side, I was lucky because I had never borrowed any money for shares and all that kinda stuff."

There was sometimes recognition of that financial loss and a presentation of professionalism by some interviews, keen to show themselves as caring managers who had a continued role in the organ-isation as motivator and manager.

> "I always made a conscious effort right, even though I personally have lost a lot out of this, I have put a lot of time in here and I had my shares as security so as to pay off the mortgage at that point in the future. I never let that anger get out because I always said, listen I have a big team here, my duty is to manage them but at the same time, try and keep them motivated . . ."

The anger was never "let out". This suggests an appearance of acceptance, but perhaps simmering rage seeped out in other areas.

There was also acknowledgement that the financial loss that was experienced was a sign of the rewards they had benefited from in the past and their attachment and commitment to the bank in the good times.

> "We'd invested so much in the organisation and particularly the longer you were here, and we had been rewarded so much by the organisation. We were all shareholders."

The end is dawning on these interviewees. There have been good times but now they are over. Financial loss was expressed by the following interviewee, who highlights the loss of assets and reflects the context of the downfall: this bank failed as many other financial institutions failed, and his property was devalued as so many others were also devalued. There is an attitude of realism to the economic situation and almost a confessional air to the interview.

> "I suffered significant loss. I had bought property in 2006, what one might call a trophy house. Huge debt on it. Wasn't secured on the shares but I got the borrowings on the basis of my wealth in the shares because I'd never be given the mortgage on the basis of income. And I suppose I suffered a double whammy in that period because the shares have gone to zero and there's been . . . they estimated 60%, wipe down in property values across the board."

The extent of the loss and pain was something the interviewee returned to again and again: huge loss, personal loss, negative equity, carrying a significant mortgage, no bonus, no opportunity for promotion. Finally, towards the end of the interview this was expressed as a figure.

> "It was a very painful experience. Because when you lose a seven figure sum . . ."

Naming this loss in the concrete terms of the huge financial loss experienced seems a critical part of the mourning process; it is not an abstract loss or an imagining. This figure represents the shocking and huge loss, not only of the money, but also of the security and quality of life such a figure represented to the individual. The security felt by this interviewee as a result of his investment wealth was, in fact, a false wealth, a false sense of omnipotence that has led to huge personal collateral damage.

Critical to the mourning organisation is this acknowledgement of organisational death; this includes a contextualisation of the ending in terms of individual responsibility and the place of the organisation in the broader social and economic context. Freud makes a clear-cut distinction between mourning and melancholia, even suggesting that mourning is not an activity that occupies the unconscious. This demarcation is helpful, but also too clean-cut to be applied absolutely to an organisation in crisis. The mourning organisation also experiences pain and defends itself against the pain of the loss of income, status, and stability.

The value of work

Another part of mourning is the recognition of what is lost; for many at Interbank, it is the work itself that was valued and mourned. The slow closedown gave people the chance to continue to operate and function as they came to terms with the shutdown. This semblance of normality was valued, keeping busy and maintaining a working identity was recognised as positive and a means to survive.

> "To be honest, it kept people busy. It kept people interested, which I thought was important because . . . err . . . there's other people who haven't been allowed to work at their job for a year and half. And I think that's soul destroying."

The importance of work to quality of life was recognised and expressed. The following interviewee at the headquarters firm supports the notion of work in itself as valuable, even work without a future. Here in the city, in which the HQ was located, unemployment and redundancy were crippling for the population, with jobs very hard to come by, particularly in the financial service sector. "To love and to work" is often cited as Freud's tenet for a meaningful life, relevant here because it allows a fulfilling existence.

"And I deliberately probably forced myself to weigh up the prag-
matism of a, of actually getting paid every month, or just going
and then getting my life back . . . err . . . and a career back particularly. But life as well because they are intertwined."

Some made a conscious decision so look on the bright side, to
adopt a position that allowed them to maximise the difficult position
they were in and to make the most of it.

"I had a simple view as well—I am going to do the best I possibly can here."

There was considerable stigma attached to working at Interbank,
this extended to the removal of external corporate branding. In the
city of the bank's headquarters, no offices had signage outside the
building; access was via a neutral security guard who discreetly
directed visitors to different offices and teams. When commuting
between offices, staff were briefed to be dropped around the corner to
the bank and to offer a vague description of where they worked. Any
other action would, it was anticipated, invite abuse and aggression.
Resignation and acceptance of the stigma was expressed by some, for
example:

"That's not the worst thing in the world, to have to lie to a cab
driver about where you're going, you know."

However, this sentiment perhaps masked something more. The
interviewee who feigned such a worked through, complete understanding of the organisation's collapse later spent three weeks off
work on sick leave. His undiagnosed illness suggested that the pain of
his working situation, presented in such a matter-of-fact manner, had
indeed taken its toll in other ways. What could not be expressed
within the organisation was taken outside of the organisation, the
collapse of his health an indication that all was not well. This "cup
half-full" thinking was expressed still further by some who even
described the situation as having some kind of silver lining:

"There is a sort of silver lining to all this, and given that we're in
wind down, we've got the time. So, to spend on ourselves, to cut
people a bit of slack when you need to."

For others, there was a realisation that the short lifespan at Inter-bank did not mean an easy ride; the situation and the work conditions were demanding and difficult. The external stigma and the knowledge of closure were also aggravated by the difficulty of the work. Getting through the work and the situation was accepted as a necessity:

> "Yeah, yeah, we're screwed, we're screwed. So I knew, like, look-ing at this and watching it and seeing what's happening, and I was, like, we're goosed. This is a very difficult place to work and the work we're doing is quite difficult and I think you have to be very strong to work here and it . . . and it's also this place has a very time-limited future as well. Like, this will mean passing time and that's it."

The working environment did not run smoothly and there were constant problems encountered with changes in management, loss of staff, and decreasing resources, coupled with additional demands from the government body overseeing the bank's closedown. This government body was targeted with recovering the best financial return for the taxpayer and monitored performance closely. It was a source of great angst to the department and the interviewees who saw the constant requests for information and monitoring as intrusive and demanding. For some, though, this micro management and reporting requirements were accepted.

> "There were body blows for the team, you know. And people still had faith, but then the last time it happened it was hands up, you know, let's just accept that it's going to be . . . err . . . going to be the end or fairly close to it now."

Acknowledgement of the situation, of the loss, was also reflected in reference to the future. There is a future without the organisation and Anna, the department head, encourages the team to focus on that and to prepare for that. The observation notes from a management meeting reflect the willingness to name the end and the need to prepare for that end.

> There is then discussion of some other development opportunities that Anna encourages the team to take—she says that the training will be useful for people when they are in new organisations in the future.

Here, the end of working life at Interbank is named and staff are urged to prepare for a working life elsewhere, an afterlife. Part of the process of mourning is the recognition of what has been lost and the value of work in the completeness and fulfilment of life. Work is acknowledged as providing a semblance of normality at difficult times. The slow closure offered employees a way of coping and of coming to terms with the end. There was evidence and recognition of the value of work.

Containing anxiety: meetings, safety, sickness, and humour

I turn now to the way in which the mourning organisation contained the anxiety of working in the climate of closure and collapse. Here, I outline the structure of containment (Bion, 1985) provided by the regular programme of meetings and the attention given to the safety of employees. The role of sickness in providing a means to cope with the pain of the situation experienced in working in a dying organisation is illustrated as well as reference to the release and place of humour.

Meetings

The bank operated a highly co-ordinated system of management meetings, departmental meetings, and team and individual reviews. Meeting rooms were constantly being booked, reports prepared, and agendas constructed. Procedures were written and rewritten, communication formalities established, and routines and procedure rigorously conducted and monitored. The management meetings that formed a regular part of the observation reflect this.

> There is a tabulated agenda and items are dealt with progressively. Anna does most of the talking. She makes a lot of jokes. She smiles and invites comments. Each person then gives a report on their "sunshine and rain". It takes me a few people's reports to realise this format. It is something the participants appear familiar with but enter into with a somewhat grudging and hesitant manner. There is a contrast between the jolly and encouraging manner of the meeting chair and the hesitant and non-spontaneous input of the participants.

The members of the meeting seem to be going through the motions. The jollity of the agenda sets a tone that does not seem to match the response of participants. Yet, all collude and go through the mechanics of participating in the meeting, reporting on their sunshine, their rain, their showers, news from their teams. The frequency and structure of the meetings seems to contain the work group and allow them to operate.

The way in which the management team controls the productivity of the team is discussed and, in particular, the use of the internet. This is allowed at lunchtime but not during any other point in the day. There is an illusion that the management team are aware of the real time use of the internet that Anna is keen not to dispel. This appears to give her a sense of control. Retaining normality and control in a potentially out of control environment appears fundamental.

> Elaine and Ricardo smile—definitely sunshine, she says, tropical sunshine, the file reviews have gone so well. Well done says Anna. She asks if it is something about being on the bottom numbers and they say no—just working well (there is a jolly and successful vibe). Syra begins by saying that never mind showers, it is soaking on her team, everyone needs their umbrellas. They are getting soaked; it has been very busy. She is animated (I have not seen her so animated before) and she says the situation is made more difficult by absences. Helen follows, oh, sunshine sunshine she says, I am fully staffed and we are getting on well.

Syra's storm passes without comment, sandwiched between reports of sunshine and success. A blind eye is turned to glimpses of struggle and lack of control. This micro activity seems to reflect the actions of the broader organisation and the City itself in the build-up to the 2008 financial crisis.

During this meeting, absences are named. Those who have departed from the team and the loss that their departure creates is articulated. Valerie follows her statement of loss with a matter-of-fact and contented description of how she is well staffed and everything is going smoothly. This contrasts with the difficulty of managing with absences, of living without loss, and living within a mourning organisation.

Safety

A second side of mourning was expressed through a preoccupation with safety. Safety was also an issue high on the management agenda.

This is reflected in the safety campaign launched to coincide with the renaming of the bank. Interbank became branded formally as New Interbank. This involved a change of logo in all common parts, even the toilets, and prominently in the safety campaign series. The attempt to create a normal working environment was illustrated with a safety campaign involving posters and online screen savers. The danger of being at work is highlighted with the New Interbank safety programme concerning the hazards of work: there is an online campaign and a series of three safety posters. The irony of the death of the organisation as the greatest hazard of all was not openly discussed, but is striking.

> I notice a third screen saver safety poster—this one has an image of a person slipping backwards and refers to Facilities' responsibility to address anything dangerous. I notice that this third safety poster sits with the first two on the large notice board. A screen saver prominently displays the New Interbank logo and an oversized red cross, "A POSITIVE safety culture helps to prevent accidents and ill health to you and your colleagues".

The organisation continues to display concern for its employees and to offer a guide to their health and safety at work, an encouragement to "take care", anything may happen. While the organisation continues, in its dying form, there still needs to be regulation, concern, and safety.

The frequency of change in layout and personnel creates an unstable environment. From one week to the next, the location of individuals and teams changes, configuration of teams and desk layout is constantly moving. As an observer, I find this unsettling, the meetings, safety, internet and sickness monitoring can be interpreted as a means to contain the anxiety caused by that constant change.

> I note that there has been a change of layout since my last visit. People have moved down the office and there is now an empty row of desks between two teams. I also note different configurations of people. The quartet that had been at my immediate right is now sitting on my left and centrally, without the same formation.

Empty desks, disappearing colleagues, unfilled spaces—this is the new normal. Even a week is a long time where consistency cannot be expected. In such an environment, the anxiety of the inevitable end was contained through the system of work activities, meetings, and business as normal initiatives. This offered a containing experience for the work group and allowed people to continue to function without crippling anxiety.

Sickness

A third issue of mourning that manifested itself was sickness. One of the symptoms of the stress of dealing with the dying organisation was a high degree of sick leave in the department. This was a regular topic of discussion at management meetings. Anna seemed somewhat resigned to the degree of sick leave taken, but the analogy of performance with sick leave being at Olympic medal-winning proportions represents her incredulity at the amount of time taken off. The detailed measurement of this performance issue continues throughout the observation period. However, there is no mention during the meetings of why sick leave is at such high levels, or any acknowledgement of the stressful working conditions. For example, as demonstrated from the following observation notes of a management meeting,

> Then there is an animated discussion about sick leave. They are on forty-two at the moment. It reached fifty-five last month. There is a lot of sighing and shrugging of shoulders. What can we do? Cost of funds to go next says Anna. Ricardo goes next: he talks about sick leave which is at record levels—Anna jokes if sick leave were an Olympic sport they would be medal winners. Forty-two days in January—that would be good if it were a target.

There is sarcasm, but also surrender to the discussion of sick leave. The physical expression of powerlessness, the shrug and the sighs indicated a lack of fight for a battle that was already lost. This struggle with a battle lost mirrors the bank's own fight for survival; a fight that has been lost. Anna literally does not know what to do to address this; it seems this is a battle she is not willing to engage in. Other examples during the observation suggested that, in order to get through the rigours and demands of the work, there needed to be a shutdown in relating to the emotional experience of the closure and the pain that it might inflict. A conversation between Anna, and Mike, a colleague who is soon leaving, illustrates this.

They talk about the dichotomy of their experience, about the sadness of leaving such great people, of the fact that he is getting emotional. Anna does not respond to this and tells him to go on to LinkedIn—then she says it will be a natural progression to Facebook, LinkedIn is like grown up Facebook, she says, but Facebook is much more fun. Oh, I don't know, he says; you'll see she says. They have a hug.

The impact of the environment on one's physical wellbeing was, however, palpable in this observation note.

The meeting is quiet and formal. All the right things are said but it feels heavy. I realise I feel very, very tired. The awful thought that I might drop off comes into my head and I pick myself up to full attention. Anna asks Elaine if she is awake. She looks so sleepy. I am fearful this message is for me. The air conditioning drones.

Here, through transference and countertransference, the weight of the working environment is felt and expressed as exhaustion. Another observation extract confirms the strain and fatigue . . .

Save the exact figures for COF meeting this afternoon, says Anna; it will keep me going, keep me awake.

The physical strain of the working environment is reflected in the high rate of sickness and the evidence of fatigue. Mourning can be described as a healthy way to process loss, but even a healthy processing of loss involves pain and discomfort. The sickness in Interbank illustrates the way in which it allowed individuals to manage their suffering; if it could not be expressed at work, it could manifest itself somatically in sickness.

Humour

Finally, humour was evident throughout and deemed to be very important in the mourning process. Anna would often wander around the desks and ask, "Anyone got something funny?" She spoke with pride of the different atmosphere on her floor and in other departments. The need to keep a sense of fun was evident, even if this was at her expense.

She catches sight of Ricardo laughing. Why are you laughing she asks? Oh its just BJ's moustache says Ricardo. I know, BJ says, it is very funny. I have been growing it for a month and this is all I have. An eighteen-year-old kid I know has much better growth. Anna jokes that she has not shaved her legs for the month and that the hair is now sticking through her tights, and they are 80 denier. There is some laughter in the room. You've got to laugh says Anna—that's all we've got left.

Another joke, again at her expense, hints at the disbelief of moving through life stages, not being youthful any longer. Losing her fertility, when she still shops at ASOS, still has a student card, surely not! Anna is driven to keep the atmosphere jolly, to be smiling as the ship sinks.

There is a joke somewhere from Anna about being too young for hot flushes; someone who shops at ASOS and gets a student discount can't be getting hot flushes.

In the headquarters, efforts to bring fun and life to work are described. A weekly quiz that is a relief from the drudgery is not welcomed by all. Again, this manager insists, you have got to have a laugh.

"We had a quiz here ... ummm ... every Friday afternoon for fifteen minutes. Another department that's on the floor came over and gave up because we were just too noisy. And they ... would you just go away, I hear you but actually just go away, just look miserable, let us have a laugh for fifteen minutes on a Friday, you know."

Managing the difficulty of the situation was moderated through humour, by laughing in the face of adversity. The Fantasy Football league that took central place on the notice board on the end wall of the open plan office hints at the need for playfulness, a way out of the reality of the demise. Being entertained as the organisation collapsed was an important coping mechanism, reminiscent of the quartet playing on as the Titanic sank.

We have seen the need to contain anxiety (Klein, 1984b[1940], 1948) in the organisation and the way in which that was done through a regular schedule of meetings, through a concentration on safety at work and through the relief of sickness and humour, tools applied in mourning to cope with the pain of loss at work. It was hard for employees to reconcile the behaviour of senior management.

"We face oblivion; they face perhaps a rosy future."

The sense of them and us comes across strongly in this quote. The opposing outcomes of the leaders and the followers who had been so loyal and devoted to them appear damning. The fallibility and imperfection of the leadership team was accepted by a smaller minority of those interviewed. There was an acknowledgement of the frailty and mistakes of those in charge and a sense of being unable to change the past and, therefore, an ability to accept things as they were. This is not to say that this was a blind acceptance; those who were compliant largely expressed a strong emotional response to the crisis, but were able to move beyond their loss and to see it as a stage of their careers, as opposed to the end.

"The biggest challenge is I think is, once you accept that and you realise that is the way it is and it's change and it . . . it's not going back to what it was."

The leaders were not seen as perfect: their management approach, which had been to give people a great deal of freedom in making as much profit as possible for the bank, with very few questions asked, was acknowledged. People who had been used to being autonomous and powerful were being told to leave their posts.

"This was a particularly difficult job that needed to be done. Umm . . . and it involved having to get rid of people who had never been really managed in the last fifteen years."

There was acknowledgement of the personal responsibility of individuals in the bank's downfall. The organisation had operated in a manner that gave staff freedom and creativity to conduct their affairs; this collusion in flexible and unregulated working became the way they did things and the consequences of the lack of regulation were disastrous. Personal accountability for colluding with the system of profiteering and capital gain is acknowledged here. As one interviewee expresses it,

"Actually, funnily enough, when I came in here, basically I was very critical of the set-up as it was. But . . . umm . . . to be fair to people here, they gave me the rope to put around my neck and then hang myself."

The way in which the leaders empowered staff to manage independently and to believe in their ability to achieve greatly was something this employee warmed to, despite initial resistance. Although he describes the freedom as being essentially freedom to destroy himself, this reference to suicide is not fantastical. Several Interbank employees did indeed commit suicide. Despite the freedom to operate freely and with autonomy, some were able to acknowledge that, in the crisis of closure, management decisions would not always be unanimously popular or desirable, as one interviewee states: "There's no point crying about it."

Rather than anger and bitterness, there is a sentiment expressed here of understanding. The senior man did not choose the path this individual would have done, but there is recognition from him that this is often what occurs in any organisation. This is a sentiment also expressed in the City of London with regard to the way in which responding to different leadership style presents a challenge:

"Maybe we are all on a shorter fuse or something, we all kind of juggle many different masters."

Acknowledgement of the end and mourning does not indicate that such an ending was easy—the harsh reality of identity loss is expressed keenly in the headquarters office. What could and could not be accepted was well thought through by some.

"You can accept losing a lot of money. What you can't accept is losing some of your fundamental status. I worked hard all my life, a lot of education, to think it could be wiped out; you know you're on the breadline as a bankrupt."

What emerged was the personal loss as the object that was mourned. Leadership and management had disappointed, but there was, from some, an acknowledgement of their fallibility and the benefits of their leadership and management styles in the past. The behaviour of the senior managers was, for some people, and in some ways, reconciled.

Reparation

For some Interbank employees, there was a sense of working through the anger and bitterness. There was not a climate or expression of blind acceptance of the fate of the bank or their personal future, but, once acknowledged, there was the ability of some to let go of the anger.

> "Well I think there is bitterness. Yes, so, I can't deny that there is bitterness. But you've got to move on. I've been thinking you can't change what's happened in the past. You can only influence what happens in the future."

In accepting the situation of the organisation's closure and the loss of status and money, there was a recognition that worse things can happen. Some accepted the boom and bust and considered their best options, leaving on their own terms with a redundancy package, for example. There was some evidence of perspective in the light of the crisis and the balance of what really is important for the interviewee. One interviewee talks of his sick wife, who he says is what is important.

> "I have a wife who's been ill over the last . . . last number of years. She's had cancer a number of different times. Now she's getting through it and she's in good health at the moment. But this is . . . that is more important."

His slip of the tongue at the end of the interview hints that what is most important is not necessarily so clear-cut. His wife's health is paramount but this collapse is important, too.

The following extract highlights the stages that people moved through to reach an expressed acceptance and the ability to progress, to move on.

> "Anger is probably the first thing. So, sort of people are in denial and then they're angry that we were lied to, that we were cheated, that people took our money. So that and I think the anger was nearly directly proportional to the length of service. So the longer you've been here, the angrier you were. Whereas someone who

was here for two years is sort of going well, that's life. So I think there's a huge amount of anger and then I'd say there was resentment after that, rather than acceptance. Because people then resented people who were involved in what happened, that they were still here. So they're angry first of all and then there's resentment. And gradually there was acceptance. Then they could sort of go, you move on."

This interviewee rationalises the process of loss and offers an uncomplaining face. Perhaps the research interview itself was a means of presenting himself as someone who could "move on", someone able to process the loss in a logical and understanding manner. Perhaps this, too, was a stage in mourning the lost organisation. The mourning organisation, therefore, displays the characteristics of the depressive position. It is able to hold the good and the bad of the closedown and to integrate both of these experiences.

There was some recognition that the corporation had created problems that were felt beyond the confines of the organisation itself and did ricochet into the broader community and society.

"I think in terms of working here now it's a very difficult place to work and it's difficult because there's a certain amount of what are we doing this for? Well, we're doing this almost like, you know, on one level you could say it's . . . we're in some small way working off a debt we owe this society."

Bion's work on basic assumption group behaviour and sophisticated work group behaviour (1961), in line with depressive position thinking (Klein, 1984b[1940]) is relevant here. Bion's assumption is that work groups, despite their attempts to pursue sensible and realistic goals, do, from time to time, fall into madness, a state which he refers to as basic assumption function. The mourning organisation has avoided this psychotic functioning. I have shown that, from the perspective of some of the employees, the mourning organisation is able to function as a work group (Bion, 1961) and, although there is a process of working through required, there is an ability to integrate the anxiety and stress of loss and emerge as a functioning work group. The activities described were not just individuals going through a mourning process, but an expression of the system as a whole.

The organisation experienced reparation as a result of working through the paranoid–schizoid position and emerged able to tolerate the organisation in its totality: an organisation that had provided good times and good income, but an organisation that was also responsible for loss of income and security. This integration of the whole object, which can be named as reparation, in Kleinian terms, is, I would suggest, for Freud, a mourning organisation.

Summary

The mourning exhibited by employees has been explored and the question of what characterises a normal response to organisational death has been examined. Some, those with less emotional investment and attachment to the organisation, such as the short-term contract workers, seemed able to "use their time well", to be able to absorb the benefits of the experience of working in crisis, and to build their skill and knowledge base as a consequence. The chapter has shown how this acceptance of loss was worked through and the recognition of the value of work, no matter how limited, was significant. The structure of the organisation, with regular meetings, close management control, safety concerns, and sickness monitoring, were shown to be the means of containing the anxiety of those facing the end. Humour also played its part.

I have also shown that, for some, there was a reconciliation of the behaviour of senior managers, an acceptance and working through of disappointment and broken promises that led to reparation. The mourning organisation has been likened to an organisation occupying the depressive position (Klein, 1952) and operating with the capacity to think and control its anxiety, as a sophisticated work group (Bion, 1961). I have quoted in the chapter from individual interviewees and from my observations. I see the individuals cited and the groups observed as mutually dependent. While individuals speak for themselves, they also say something for the wider system of which they are part (Armstrong, 2005; Bion, 1961). Where it might be difficult to see disturbance in individuals, such elements of disturbance in the group and wider organisation can be seen more clearly.

A Freudian notion of mourning is, therefore, relevant and helpful in understanding organisational death (Freud, 1917e). Mourning has been linked to the depressive position where whole object integration allows the good and bad in organisation and leadership to be tolerated. Bion's (1961) work on groups has extended the thinking to incorporate basic assumption behaviour and the sophisticated work group. An organisation facing closure might respond in a healthy, mournful way, but could equally display pathological symptoms of melancholia, which is dealt with in the next chapter.

CHAPTER FIVE

Melancholia at work

"The distinguishing mental features of melancholia are a profoundly painful dejection, cessation of interest in the outside world, loss of the capacity to love, inhibition of all activity, and a lowering of self-regarding feelings to a degree that finds utterance in self-reproaches and self-revilings and culminates in a delusional expectation of punishment"

(Freud, 1917e, p. 244)

The melancholic organisation exhibits pathological responses to organisational death and is unable to cope with its ending. Its members, in addition to the painful symptoms of loss associated with mourning, are also encumbered with a depletion of self-esteem and a deep depression. The melancholic organisation goes beyond the anticipated response to death and incorporates the self at the centre of painful loss. Self-reproach and self-reviling are not present in mourning. In mourning, attacks are directed to the outside world, whereas in melancholia the attacks are directed inward, loss is harder to compute, and, rather than being worked through, are trapped inside and become a self-persecuting internal object.

When the ego is depleted, no matter how benevolent the organisation or the behaviour of the leaders and managers might be, there is no possibility of responding to overtures, such as career counselling or coaching sessions. Whatever the organisation does, it could never be enough. The melancholic is unable to acknowledge his loss, yet cannot express this consciously; his self-esteem is damaged but he cannot pinpoint his loss. In the case of the melancholic, the object loss is transformed into an ego-loss. The injustice of the loss, the way in which the individual has been let down, manifests itself initially as revolt—the object has disappointed the individual—which then translates into a crushed sense of melancholia (Freud, 1917e; Frosh, 2012).

Freud helps us to see that the split off parts of the ego that the melancholic attacks, and the accusations made against himself, are actually an attack on the lost loved object. This is a helpful way of examining employees' responses to organisational endings. Personal reproach and condemnation, depression and blame are directed inwards, yet these attacks are actually directed to the lost object, the loved organisation that has betrayed the individual by failing and, therefore, leaving him. The laments against such employees, therefore, are actually accusations aimed at the organisation.

Freud describes three preconditions for melancholia: the loss of the object; ambivalence, and the regression of the libido into the ego. He suggests that when the work of melancholia is concluded, mania emerges.

Each element of melancholia is addressed: painful dejection; lowering of self-regard, loss of the loving object, an expectation of punishment, and cessation of interest in the outside world. We encounter a sense of the organisation from the inside, a private perspective of collapse.

Melancholic loss

Loss was expressed universally by those interviewed and was made more profound by their previously held conviction of their immortality, a belief that they were too good, too clever, and too successful to fail. Trust in their leaders and surety of their brilliance led to an arrogance of self-belief, that with continued work, their star would continue to rise and the organisation would remain a brilliant and revered institution. There were feelings of despair and dejection, justifying their otherwise self-described strong and capable characters and illustrating just how painful the prospect of the end was for them.

> "So I think it's just about ... sometimes when you hear things that maybe hit your Achilles heel, no matter how good you get at dealing with that stuff, you still have to go through the cycle pit of despair, and that whole thing, where you have go 'hang on, hang on a minute'!"

Employees struggled to absorb the reality of closure and ending, as melancholics fail to connect with the lost objects and work through their loss. Some struggled to function, to continue with the activity expected of them.

> "I think it's been a really painful period for a lot of people because ... it's been a great test of people's resilience. And some people just couldn't handle the dysfunctional nature of things. And you know, again the old Interbank, as people would fondly describe it, would have been very much a meritocracy. You could argue quite a ruthless meritocracy."

Loss of reputation and pride was another strong trope running through the dialogue, a sense of the mighty fallen and shock and dismay at their fall from grace, almost disbelief. Alongside this loss was suffering and pain, an emotional and crushing experience for individuals who had believed their own hype and had not anticipated their end. There was despair, shock, and pain associated with the employee's loss.

> "It was like we fell off a cliff."

The description shows the dramatic visceral nature of the organisation's closure, making the loss one that was indeed very hard to bear.

Lowering of self-regard

Employees joined an organisation full of hope and with the certainty of a bright future. They invested great aspirations into the organisation and its failure led to a consequential lowering of self-regard. Identification with the object, in this case the organisation, was extremely strong. So much was devoted and imbued into this object, and so much of their identity was tied up in belonging, its history, and the future. Employees made perhaps a narcissistic choice, working for an organisation that represented themselves—popular, creative, and successful—or possibly an aspirational ideal of themselves. To lose their futures and their dreams in this case equates to losing an object that might even be extended to a sense of losing part of oneself. With that loss was also the loss of the capacity to love the organisation that had been very much in their hearts.

The destruction of the organisation could be felt as their own demise. The public annihilation of the revered object, the stratospherically successful, bold, risk-taking, model organisation with which they were inextricably linked, was hugely painful.

"I just really, really loved the place. And of course also you had the finance benefits as well. So you'd have been paid well, and you had your bonuses, and yeah, working for a company that, everyone was jealous of you working there. You know. I know my family were very much wow, you're working at Interbank, lucky you."

There were expressions of sorrow about better times and the sad situation employees found themselves in. There was a sense that the outside world would not understand what they had been through. There was also an expression of shame as evidenced in the following observation note.

I listen to a conversation between Elaine and a visiting colleague. When Elaine joined, it was the sixth largest employer—what should she do, sell her home? Buy something smaller? Get a local job? There is a taint, don't say you work for Interbank. There are empty houses. Staff lost lots of money through shares, as Elaine did. She would not even open an Interbank umbrella. Elaine reports that she was even stopped at airport and asked why are you here? She did not say.

The collapse had forced deception on its members: they had almost to deny their existence to avoid confrontation and blame; their identity as Interbank employees had to disappear. What was less evident, however, was a sense of self-reproach, there was denial, a sense of deflation and denigration, but there was little evidence of individuals taking responsibility for the collapse. Some commented on their willingness to accept the good times, therefore they needed to accept the bad times, too, but they did not express these bad times following the good times as something for which they felt responsible. This did not move across into self-reproach at a conscious level.

Loss of the loving object

"I suppose, you know, for some it was like a death in the family."

The loss of trust emerged as a painful realisation of the lack of honesty of the leaders in whom there was faith and who were so warmly embraced by employees. Their testimony appears almost as a shock, that this news had been unanticipated and that their faith and trust had been betrayed. This loss of trust creates an inability to treat the organisation as the loving object it had been; the organisation as loving family becomes an object of abuse and betrayal.

> "So then suddenly realising that they actually hadn't been straight with you, umm, they hadn't been straight with any of us, they'd lied a lot at the time, it was a massive betrayal. It was like, yeah, them, they were your family, saying, doing something and you realise that they've lied. The trust that we had in the team and the family, it sort of really, really was crushed. And that upset a lot of people."

Many references were made to a familial feel to the organisation, that working at Interbank was like being part of an extended family. The betrayal was a familial betrayal. Freud describes the root of all groups as the family and this familial description supports the close ties members felt to each other and to the organisation.

There was also huge love and affection expressed for the leader of the bank, Jack. His ability to communicate with staff on a personal level, to know everyone's names and to show compassion when his people were suffering (an interviewee spoke of his personal support and kindness during bereavement, for example) was often expressed. This was a leader that was not only loved, but also someone with whom the employees were proud to be associated:

> "As CEO he was the most charismatic man in the entire world. But he was just, you know, you couldn't, you couldn't but love him. He was so warm. Ah, he was as hard as nails, but my god could he woo the crowds."

The members of Interbank identified strongly with the organisation and did so with considerable pride. Their identity was caught up in the reputation and status of the bank and with its collapse there was an experience of personal disintegration and loss of pride. Long (2008) suggests that corporate pride might be a new form of patriotism, and pride in the organisation was certainly evident in many of the interviews undertaken. Identity was caught up in the institution; there was reflected glory in its success and its promising future for the bright, hopeful employees who were so attached to this feted and glorious organisation.

> "We'd come from the organisation that was always based on trust, it was always based on communication. Management by walkabout, and now you had the polar opposite."

The pride was expressed in the way things were done at Interbank, the example that leaders showed in communicating clearly and openly, being accessible and trustworthy. That was all lost. This fall from grace was also attributed to the leader, who was cited as winning numerous business and personality awards and moving from being the most admired and feted leader to the most derided and hated.

> "From a professional impact then, you lose the pride that you had in working for the best bank to actually now being demonic and, you know, if you . . . if somebody says what do you work in now, I'm an accountant. I work in . . . I don't say I work for Interbank or I don't even say I work in a bank. Whereas before I would have been, I work at Interbank, the best bank in the world."

What had been a source of strong identification and validation became a source of shame. The pride in, attachment to, and love for the bank are expressed clearly in the above quote. The following observation of the closure gave insights into the way ritual and practice illustrated the attachment to, and loss of, the loved object, the bank and its clients.

> Various people walk past me to the glass office, carrying cardboard boxes. They take them into the glass office and walk back. There is procession of at least six boxes taken into the office. There is a slow traffic of boxes to the glass office but I note the office is open for some of the time, whereas usually it is opened with a swipe pass. One man walks his box to the office on a trolley and then wheels back the empty trolley.

My sense is that of a funeral procession, or of symbolic sacrifices being paraded across the office. Each of the boxes represents a client whose history of lending and relationship is contained within it. The association is of an urn of ashes. Also evoked is the image of the Lehman Brothers' employees who left their place of work suddenly and in shock, grasping a cardboard box containing their personal effects. The work with these clients is now finished; they are being put to rest. There is a cessation of activity.

Expectation of punishment

The intense identification with the organisation meant that individuals found the failure of the bank hard to separate from their personal failure, whether or not they attributed their behaviour as culpable or not. This paranoid–schizoid thinking, the sense that these individuals caused the failure in some way, is relevant here. The shame associated with this fallen institution led to behaviour aimed at saving face, for example, saying one is an accountant rather than a banker. The financial loss experienced by the majority of those interviewed emerged as the initial comment on the impact of the downfall on them as individuals. There were many tales of houses lost, shares devalued, and lifestyles altered dramatically. The personal loss of income and lifestyle was commented on, as well as the loss of the future that many had assumed would be buffered by the comfort of financial success.

The financial ruin experienced was a powerful factor that had an impact on their work, home, and internal life. Interviewees spoke of dream homes burdened by huge mortgages, now significantly reduced in value, of lifestyle changes and of the long-term grind of repaying the debts that they had been left with. The prospect of bankruptcy loomed heavily for others, and with that financial loss came many other features of loss, including the shame of careers crushed and the loss of hope in the future that had been so firmly clung to. There was also reference to the loss of reward for their hard work and efforts.

> "It hits at a personal level obviously in terms of financial, because like a lot of people I had a lot of bank stock and would have been comfortable. So that financial bedrock is now gone. So I have a labour of love for the next twenty years to clear off whatever I owe."

The consequences of the collapse, the fall from grace, left those involved in the collapse very angry. It was recognised that people benefited from a good lifestyle and financial success during the good times. But their expectation that these good times would continue was evident and its failure to do so a cause of contempt and fury. They would have to pay a heavy price for buying into the dream of Interbank.

> "Quite honestly, you know, people had bought shares and done incredibly well and had lived a very good lifestyle because it was seen as a very good punt. And over a period of twenty years people did very well out of it. But it collapsed and so, you know, there were a lot of very angry people."

The bank was an object of aggression and identification with Interbank was something that members were keen to keep their distance from. It was only when the bank was renamed that people were able to speak once more of the place that employed them. Employees expected to be punished by association.

There was a sense of reincarnation with the rebranding exercise. Every notice, plaque, and screensaver was retitled "New Interbank". In this reincarnation, the organisation could avoid the punishment it was due and be reborn, with a fresh start.

> I notice that the New Interbank logo is everywhere, at the entrance to the building, on the security pass, on the safety posters, notice boards,

even on the back of the toilet door. But, as I look closely at the desks and office furniture, I note the old branding—Interbank—small but indelible on every fixture and fitting in my eyeline. I also notice a small bar code label on my desk, then also notice it on all the others and the filing cabinets, saying Interbank. But New Interbank is on the screen, notice board, back of the toilet door even.

The inability to escape the history and identity of the bank is reflected in the above observation. A corporate decision can be made to rebrand, to present itself differently to the outside world, but if one looks carefully the identity is there to be seen. It is not easy to rid the organisation of its name: traces remain.

Indeed, the logo was removed from all public buildings and visitors to the bank explained that they often asked to be dropped around the corner from the address so that they could avoid confrontation and abuse.

The taint of working at Interbank was not purely fantasy; the employees were directed to keep the place of their employment close to their chests. If they said where they worked, they could expect abuse and derision. This was a dramatic change for employees who had held their place of work in such high esteem and had been so proud to be associated with Interbank. The scramble for corporate goods seems a nostalgic exercise, a means of holding on to the glory of the past.

"You remember the name you were so proud to say and now it's kind of disappeared, you know. Everyone . . . we had a whole lot of cups and umbrellas and the usual things that you'd have. And I think they brought them down to the first floor and everyone just had a free-for-all, for what they wanted. And people, a lot of people were saying they were collectors' items, you know, for a company that no longer exists. A different name."

The fear and pain of death is expressed by a young woman whose comments on her mother's death appear to come unexpectedly, and perhaps, speaks to the loss experienced by the team.

Then a woman says, my mother's dying and I have to bury her. There is a puzzled response. She says it again. Then she says if my mum dies, I die. Then there is quiet.

It is too much perhaps for them to face, the truth of death and closure; this woman speaks for the organisation closing down.

Cessation of interest in the outside world

There is lethargy and a lack of energy observed and expressed. The members are going through the motions, but their heart is not in it. During the uncertain times and drawn out process of closure there were a variety of plans for the bank's survival that reached employees; while some dismissed any reason to be attached to an organisation that would no longer exist in the foreseeable future, others remained hopeful that one or other of the schemes would lead to another bright new future.

"The organisation is being wound down, whether it takes five, ten, fifteen, twenty years it's going. So why would people be totally loyal to it? There's nothing in it for them."

The loss appears compounded by the pride in the open culture and communication practice of the organisation in the past. People felt that they were well informed and up to date with happenings in the company. There is almost a disbelief that they are not being told what is happening.

"Interbank was an organisation that was culturally very open, it was very transparent. People knew what was going on generally. They generally knew what was happening and therefore when there was no communication, it felt odd and it felt different."

The organisation functioned differently, activity was conducted in a functional vein, rather than the energetic and dynamic operation it had defined itself as. There was no interface with the outside world, or open communication and dialogue. The slow closure was relevant to the way in which people responded to the organisation's death, as Freud (1915) identifies, it is impossible to imagine our death, as, when we do so, we are forever present as spectators. It is the same with the organisation facing closure. The employees were still there months, even years, after the announced closure, thereby perpetuating the notion of the organisation's immortality.

> "We had our crash. Then there was a new management team appointed. And at that point the vision was there would be a good bank and a bad bank. So you'd strip all the bad stuff and park it over there. And nobody really was going to figure out who's going to run that. But of course everybody wanted to be part of the big bright new future."

This description of survival is in tune with Kleinian notions of splitting, of separating the breast into the good, all-giving source of life, and the bad breast, evil and destructive (Klein, 1946). There was also a negative side of a slow closure expressed. In mourning, the organisation goes through a process of repair and healing. In melancholia, the wound is left open. For Interbank, the wound was left open for a prolonged period; the interviewee below expresses a frustration that it was not dealt with more efficiently and expediently.

> "Having said that, they're doing a really bad job of closing it quick enough. They could do it much more effectively if . . . if they'd a better team of people in and . . . I think it could have been done with a lot less pain for staff. And it, you know, they would have been further down the road."

Timing was not in the control of those working in the bank, this was a right withheld from them. They could not choose to cash in their shares at a time to suit them, to retire at a time in life that was most conducive to their personal circumstances, or to find a new job in the time they chose. Their ending was forced upon them; the terms of the ending were anything but their own.

Some, in addition to their own roles, were faced with the task of presenting and justifying the bank's action to the outside world. Here, there was reference to break points, moments when the pressure of the situation mounted to such an extent that they felt it was impossible to carry on with the intensity and burden of the collapse.

> "Sunday morning my wife dropped me off to work and I got out the car and I started crying. And I just said I can't do this any more. I'm done."

This executive was pushed to the edge and felt he could no longer present the organisation and its complexities to the outside world. The constant pressure internally and externally led him to break point. He no longer cared what the outside world thought of him or the bank. He was done.

Others were simply unable to move on, they held within them the glory of the organisation and their success and strength in that glory; this was internalised and they simply could not accept that their leaders had betrayed them and that the end was nigh.

"I didn't really think of the next step along from Interbank. It was always I am staying with Interbank. Umm, because they had everything. And actually, if you look at it now, it was a bit of a utopia, umm, because you had, you know, you know, great people you were working with, a real kind of, umm, you get a lot of people who are very go-getting, very passionate."

Individuals presented a melancholic response to the organisation's end, evidenced in their lack of interest in the outside world.

Summary

Freud does not speak of mourning or melancholia in organisational terms; in this chapter, I have extended the theory from the ego to the group and to the organisation in discussing the melancholic organisation.

The ability to integrate the good and punishing/destructive sides of the bank was impossible. Individuals were unable to cope with the loss of the organisation and became inward looking, losing interest in the outside world.

A feature of melancholia is the fantasy of the retrievable object and the notion of a return to past glory. This was represented by a "stuckness" of some of the participants in the research who saw themselves as true believers in the charisma and potential of their leaders and their organisation. This belief might have been fuelled by the absence of an abject apology that contradicted the strongly held view of the charismatic leader as a man of the people, who cared deeply about each member of staff.

In the melancholic organisation, members were unable to embrace the end positively and adopted a denial of both the bleak circumstances and any reward or pleasure in their remaining time. The mobilisation of basic assumption activity (dependence on the idealised and revered leader and organisation, the pairing of the executives with the leadership in union against the outside world, and the fight/flight mechanism of defending their behaviour, or running from the reality of their dishonest malpractice) demonstrates Interbank's work group behaviour.

The element of melancholia that presented itself least was that of self-reproach. There was considerable reference to other elements of melancholia, to a lack of interest in the outside world, a lowering of self-regard, and an expectation of punishment, but there was little suggestion of self-blame expressed. I posit that this absence in the interviews may well have been a thought too painful to share. For most, the research offered a first opportunity to talk of their experience of the organisational death in a contained space; perhaps with further interviews and discussion, the subject of self-reproach might have emerged.

Melancholia leads to struggle and the failure of the possibility of recognition of the loss, cutting off the opportunity to move forward, beyond the loss. The chapter determines that Freud's distinction between mourning and melancholia can be useful to organisational death and contemporary organisations facing closure. Where there are signs of a melancholic response to loss, this can be acknowledged and examined, communicating to employees an awareness of the different possibilities in dealing with loss and the strong ties and identification to work that recognises organisational death as a painful bereavement.

Some suggest melancholia is an obsolescent term for what is now called depression (Rycroft, 1995). I argue that melancholia is a current and relevant term to be applied to organisational death. A melancholic organisation carries features of depressive illness and psychosis, its low spirits and self-reproach bear witness to an organisation that has become stuck in its loss and is unable to move forward.

CHAPTER SIX

The death drive

T his chapter explores the death drive and draws on the data gathered to explore the insights of Thanatos to understand organisational closure. It describes the death drive as a return to an earlier, inorganic state; it is also associated with violence, with a wish to cancel and to destroy. The chapter explains how the death drive operates in the closure of Interbank in all its vicissitudes. It compares the application of the death drive in the City of London with that in the international headquarters. The different expressions of the death drive, dissolution, and destruction are contrasted.

The death drive is expressed psychically in envy in the wish to take away something desirable that another person possesses. In the competitive environment of the City, envy, the desire to take away and destroy that which belongs to others, was seen to manifest itself (Klein, 1957). The compulsion to repeat mistakes in the world of finance and the cycle of boom and bust that epitomises the City of London is emphasised.

The violence associated with the destructive elements of the death drive are apparent, particularly expressed in the bank's head-quarters. It is important to stress that, while this aggression might have manifested itself externally in the organisation's international headquarters, with marches, fire, and public outcries, anger was also experienced in the City of London. Defences were employed to mask this rage, yet it did still emerge. Interviewees complained that they were being included in the blanket denigration of "fat cat bankers" when they were not traders and did not earn million pound bonuses. There were cries of "We work hard for our money", and such cries were commonplace.

Eros and Thanatos can both express themselves in the behaviour of leaders and others in an organisation. At a vulnerable time of loss, particularly when the organisation had been thought of as vibrant, even immortal, so much more so. We see in the expression of mourning and melancholia the pain of losing the loved object. With Thanatos, hateful and aggressive feelings are given expression. Where the leader was idealised and loved in the melancholic organisation, in the world of Thanatos the leader is destroyed. Aggression and envy is mobilised by the death drive. The compulsion to repeat, envy, aggression, and hatred—this is the death drive at work. "In a boom envy, in a bust, anger" (Lawson, 2009).

Within this chapter, we see how the death drive gives expression to the unconscious in the world of work. Chapter Two offered a comprehensive introduction to the death instinct, first presented by Freud in *Beyond the Pleasure Principle* (1920g). Freud differentiates, in this development of his theory, two drives: the sexual drive that works to achieve a renewal of life, through the libido (Eros), and the drive to death, the *mortido destrudo*, the instinct towards death (Thanatos). Later, in *Civilization and its Discontents* (1930a), Freud developed the more aggressive side of the death instinct. In this chapter, we examine the death drive in both its manifestations: as a wish to dissolve and annihilate oneself and, in its more destructive form, as a wish to kill others.

The financial world in boom times offered Interbank remarkable opportunities for success, recognition, and financial reward. Its trajectory was experienced as unstoppable and employees held the organisation, and the part they played in it, in high esteem. They were envied and admired. This awe and reverence turned to anger and destruction, as evidenced in this chapter. The editor of the *Independent* newspaper quoted (Lawson, 2009), offers a psychoanalytic interpretation (intentional or otherwise) of the response of the City to boom and bust. He identifies the primal responses to crisis of envy and aggression that are evident in an examination of the death drive at work at Interbank.

Freud began with a conflict *with* the ego and ended his theoretical examination with a conflict *within* the ego, the struggle of the part of the ego that wishes to stay alive and the part of the ego that wishes to destroy itself (Simmel, 1944). The anti-libidinal, self-destructive death instinct presented itself towards the end of Freud's life.

In organisational closure, the death drive directs the psychological activities of the mind, captured in a wish to return to an inorganic state. As a framework for understanding responses to closure or shut-down the death drive, as a desire to return to a previous state, is both relevant and helpful. It shows how a wish to return to nothingness is played out in an organisational setting. The death instinct aims to take what is living and lead it to its inorganic state, to undo connections and to destroy things (Freud, 1940e). It also demonstrates the aggressive element of the death drive, manifested in the drive of financial institutions "to pursue, relentlessly and without exception, its own self-interest, regardless of the harmful consequences it might cause to others" (Bakan, 2005, p. 2).

The chapter also illustrates how envy plays out in the demise of an organisation, and the way in which this helps to elucidate the death drive. Where this extends to the death drive is the part of envy that not only acknowledges that which the other has, that is not part of the self, but harbours the wish to destroy, or place ill will, towards the more fortunate being. This desire to do damage to another distinguishes envy from the anxiety, and defences against those anxieties.

Klein (1957) extends this concept of envy to show that this ill will is often unconscious and, further, that this ill will is often directed most powerfully towards those on whom one is dependent. For Klein, this is the mother, and the baby's envious attack on the good and life-fulfilling breast. The violent attack on the other, on whom one is dependent, is, therefore, not concerned with self-preservation.

Freud's development of the death drive was conceived after the First World War and partly in response to the dreams of returning soldiers who might today be described as suffering from post traumatic stress disorder. The compulsion to repeat traumatic experiences was identified at this point in history and its applicability to the constant repetition of boom and bust in the City of London and the global financial markets is highly relevant.

The death drive is considered as an anti-life instinct, with destructive potential to destroy the good object; the link to Klein's descriptions of envy is made clear. Its presentation as a return to nothingness is illustrated in the retreat from the crisis and the immersion in the rhythm of City life, a means to withdraw to a restful and infantile state. This chapter shows how a return to nothingness, destruction, and envy were played out at Interbank.

The chapter concludes that the death drive, expressed in both its aggressive and passive forms, was evidenced during the bank's closure and offers psychoanalytic insights into organisational closure. These insights include: the compulsion to repeat, envy, and the expression of violence—internally and externally.

How an organisation dies

The death drive manifests itself in organisational death in a number of ways. In the compulsion to repeat self-destructive behaviours, the organisation fails to recognise the disastrous consequences of continuing as they had always done, creating personal loss and corporate downfall. This is the destructive side of the death drive at work. Here envy, aggression, and mania manifest themselves with the violent montage of burning cars, marches, effigies burnt, and attacks received with shame.

In the presentation of the death drive that causes the organisation to retreat, and to turn in on itself, we see buildings and locations hidden. The identity and name that once brought pride is blocked out and rubbed away. The organisation soothes itself with a continuous hum of procedure and practice that lead nowhere as there is nowhere to go. Large, open-plan offices slowly reduce in number and occupancy until there is no one left, only the empty vessel. Freudian ideas work together; one concept does not supersede another and can work side by side. As the dualistic model of sex and narcissism developed into the model of sex and death, this did not mean that narcissism was irrelevant. So, in the two manifestations of the death drive, the violence of the death drive does not supersede the drive to the inorganic state. They coexist, as evidenced by the swing of the death drive in Interbank's two locations.

The swing of the death drive

There were different presentations of the death drive in the head-quarters and City of London research sites. The focus of my research was a single entity, the organisation, Interbank. Yet, within that entity, there was a split response to elements of the closure. This was reflected in the two sites of the research, the City of London where the observation was conducted and half the interviews took place and the international headquarters, outside of the UK, where the other half of the interviews were conducted. It became apparent that the organisation presented itself quite differently in these two locations and that the headquarter offices and the City of London base were very much separate parts of the whole system. I propose that the loss of the institution was experienced differently in these two locations and this difference reflects the oscillating position of the death drive.

Of course, the data did not present itself in a completely neat format: there were nuances and there was ambiguity. There were elements of rage, anger, and disappointment expressed in the City of London offices. There was also some acknowledgement in the headquarters interviews that personal action was at least partially responsible for the depth of individual losses. However, the flavour of the two locations was palpably different.

As an outsider on the boundary of the organisation, I had expected to see levels of conflict and anger expressed during my observation in the City of London that were not evident superficially. The response to the impending closure led these City workers to employ defensive behaviour, to protect them from the pain of their losses, suggesting a lack of aggression that was merely simmering below the surface. There was a quiet retreat and acknowledgement demonstrated. In the HQ, the tempo and flavour of each interview was more raw, possibly closer to the heart of the damage created.

As a researcher, I was also subject to the death drive. The organisation ultimately did not want to see or think of me; it "disappeared" me or, perhaps, annihilated me. The death drive was expressed in the research process; the researcher returned to nothing.

The HQ interviews offered a highly visceral experience of the end. This included several violent descriptions and a high degree of aggression and fury against those that were responsible for the downfall. This is illustrated well by the example offered of a team who collected £8,000 to bid for an old car of the CEO so that they could crush it.

> "Yeah he was arrested and he was vilified and . . . I think they paid on eBay . . . ummm . . . eight grand for his car or something just so they could crush it; it was an old car of his. You know, so that . . . you know really . . . you know, a complete hate figure. So, gone from the absolutely everyone loves him to . . . to a complete hate figure."

This act is a powerful expression of the rage and violence that the members of staff felt. These were individuals who had lost a great deal of money and yet were willing to pay thousands of pounds for the pleasure of destruction. The symbolism of his fall from grace is epitomised in the above quote; yet, even in describing this act, there was still a reticence to blame him wholly—there is a suggestion that others would have done the same. The grim reality of the corrosive management style is still not something this interviewee appears willing to acknowledge. Or, perhaps, it was simply too much to bear. The repetition of the phrase "complete hate figure" is telling and the expression of it in relation to the love and adoration previously felt adds further substance to the power of these sentiments. Others felt free to act out their anger, those that bought and burnt the car, for instance, symbolically destroying the engineer of their downfall. Expressed in this vignette is a revelling in the leader's downfall and a distance from that downfall, an identification with, and disassociation from, the death drive itself.

Outside of the formal interviews, people also spoke to me about effigies of the leader that were constructed, hung on lampposts, and burnt. It appeared, from the tales told, that these acts were carried out by both members of the public and members of staff. Freud claims that no individual can be slain in their absence: for, after all, nobody can be slain *in absentia* (Freud, 1912–1913, p. 28), yet these actions say much about the wish to exact a bloody revenge.

These acts of violence by the members of the public are a clear indication of the hatred and fury of a people let down and devastated. There was also reference to marches and public demonstrations, noisy and threatening violence. From the City of London offices, the following observation vignette shows the awareness of the power of destruction, played out in the tragedy of suicide:

They move on to the next agenda item. The planned meeting cancelled due to adverse weather conditions in the HQ office. At first Anna thought this was a joke, and then she discovered that two people had died. Not Interbank people, says Ajay? No, but two Interbank people did commit suicide. When, asks Helen? Recently, says Anna. Then she moves things swiftly along quickly to instruct Syra to mark the report not filed for reasons other than the team. The meeting ends.

The above vignette from an observation indicates the unwillingness of the management team to discuss the deep despair of their colleagues and the impact of the bank's downfall. Business as usual was the order of the day and the subject of suicide was not going to be pursued. Perhaps too painful to engage in, this devastating news is almost ignored; the manager leads the team into retreat. The suicide of two colleagues who, in desperation, took their own lives is the ultimate self-destruction, yet this was given only cursory attention; the manager and team could not face this element of the death drive at work, so their approach was to retreat to the machinations of the working day. I note, too, that, in writing up my observation notes, I also collude with the clipped attention to these horrifying details. It is only on a second and third return to the notes that I identify my own unconscious defences, mirroring those of the organisation. I know, but I also do not want to know, that the circumstances have caused so much anguish that people have taken their lives voluntarily. At another management meeting, the reluctance to go to dark and cold places is expressed in another way:

Anna puts her head into the allocated meeting room and says she will not go in there—it's too cold. We go instead to a meeting room 4, but only after Dick has gone ahead first to check the temperature. Yes, it is warm, he decrees.

The temperature of the meeting rooms is a subject that occurs often at the beginning of management meetings. There is a desire on behalf of the team to get the temperature right for Anna and a desire to control (the heat) from Anna. This is something that she can manage; she will draw the line at sitting in a cold meeting room. Her first mention of the temperature drew associations of the cold morgue. Yet, Anna perhaps is trying at least to keep herself and her team warm; she cannot protect their survival but she can at least ensure they are comfortable.

Another vignette suggests a way of escaping the reality of the closure through a retreat and escape into literature. The pairing of these two employees, one more passionate and enthusiastic than the other, hints at her desire to get away from the inevitability and dullness of working in a condemned organisation.

> Immediately, I notice new faces and a greater degree of activity than at my previous visit. Scott has moved to the corner desk of the adjacent bank of desks and appears to be working alone. Behind him is a new pair of workers—a young, nubile woman with exaggerated movement and bouncy big breasts is coaching a younger blonde man and going through some accounts with a highlighter pen. She turns to talk to Scott and I hear her say something about Homer. He says he has read *The Iliad* and she says he should read Odysseus also. She then turns to him very attentively and with enthusiasm to talk of other literature she can recommend. She seems very excited by this. Scott says OK but don't give me too many recommendations, it will be too much for me.

This woman persists in her conversation with Scott; she is keen to establish a rapport with him. She seems excited to have found someone with whom she can share her passion for literature. It is interesting that rather than referring to *The Odyssey*, she refers to Odysseus. Odysseus, known for his brilliance, his cunning, his cruelty, and his guile, is a leader whose qualities are reminiscent of the leader of Interbank, who led the bank to its destruction. I must also consider that it might have been my own "hearing", a countertransference phantasy intruding. It might well be that I heard Odysseus and she referred to *The Odyssey*, in line with her literary conversation.

Scott displays a retreat from this attempted pairing: stop, he seems to be saying, this is too much for me. This failed seduction is also reminiscent of the call of the sirens; Odysseus manages to resist the enticing call of the sirens by tying himself to the mast. Scott uses words rather than rope, but halts the seduction none the less. The encounter speaks of the libidinal energy behind Freudian theory: the research focuses on Death and the City, but Sex and the City is ever present.

The two sites, therefore, show a swing from destruction to retreat, the headquarters office more readily demonstrating the violent and aggressive elements of the death drive and the City of London site retreating, drawing back into administration, procedure, and gradually closing in towards retreat.

The two locations of the research can be viewed as expressing the death drive in two different ways. The City of London demonstrated a greater swing towards the return to nothingness, the retreat into the regular procedures, and the comfort of compliance with routine and comforting rituals. In the headquarters location, greater aggression was expressed in tales of burnt effigies, torching of cars, suicide, and threatened violence. The renaming and "hiding" of the bank was also most prominent in the headquarters.

The compulsion to repeat: boom, bust, boom, bust . . .

Central to the death drive is the compulsion to repeat, the *fort–da* that led Freud to the revision of his drive theory. In the earlier chapters, exploring "Death in theory", we see that Freud questioned the pleasure principle in a re-evaluation (1920) of *The Interpretation of Dreams* (1900a). *Beyond the Pleasure Principle* (1920g) was written soon after the First World War and after consideration of the recurring traumatic dreams of soldiers; these soldiers experienced (as mentioned) what we might term post traumatic stress disorder. Individuals repeated their dreams, again and again, in a reflex manner that suggested a compulsion to repeat beyond the pleasure principle. The death instinct is to be found in the pull towards dissolution and as an instinct of destruction.

The compulsion to repeat and the history of financial crises evidenced with regularity are core to the investigation. The collapse of markets and the cycle of boom and bust are interpreted as a manifestation of the death drive. Individuals, organisations, and markets hold a compulsion to repeat destructive mistakes again and again. This cycle of behaviour prevents proper reflection and learning and merely recreates the crisis.

Dozens of banks in the USA and Europe were engulfed in crisis during the 2008 global financial collapse. Interbank joined many others in finding itself over exposed; the scale of loss made it inevitable that many would face collapse. It is easy to view this crisis as a unique and unexpected event. However, the crisis was not only a repeat of others that had occurred in history but also could have been anticipated had warning signs been heeded. As noted during an October visit to the London School of Economics, "Why did no one see it coming?" (Queen Elizabeth II, 2008). The cycle of economic crisis and collapse suggests the compulsion to repeat is at work in the world's financial markets.

Financial crisis, followed by recession and economic slowdown, is, therefore, a pattern repeated many times since the Great Depression of the 1930s. These crises are worldwide, from South America in the 1980s, to the Nordic countries of Norway, Sweden, and Finland in the 1990s, Japan in 1991, and South East Asia in 1997. Rather than saying that the financial crisis is like nothing we have ever seen before, Krugman, the Nobel Prize winner, says,

> . . . it's like everything we've seen before, all at once: a bursting real estate bubble comparable to what happened in Japan . . . a wave of bank runs . . . a liquidity trap . . . and a wave of currency crises all too reminiscent of what happened to Asia in the late 1990s. (Krugman, 2008, p. 166)

In *Manias, Panics and Crashes* (Kindleberger & Aliber, 2011) the notion of financial crisis is identified as a hardy perennial. The behaviour of the financial markets, and those who run them, seem to be supporting Freud in his return to the compulsion to repeat in "Analysis terminable and interminable" (1937c). Here, Freud describes patients who cling to their illness and suffering, resisting every possible means of recovery. So do the markets continue to cling to their reckless boom and bust mentality. The hunger for risk and an inability to learn from past mistakes, to continue to invest in the cycle of boom, bust, and repair appears to be a feature of the financial markets, in line with the compulsion to repeat. ". . . in the event of a crisis no bank, no matter how small, can be allowed to fail. The risk is that if one bank goes, people will immediately ask: who is next?" (Darling, June 2012, cited in Perman, 2013, p. xv).

Earlier examinations of genocide provided a powerful illustration of the repetitive pattern of destruction. Following genocide, there are often cries of "never again", yet genocide continues to feature regularly in modern society. Since the establishment of the United Nations, there have been forty-five genocides and millions of deaths. Far from being unusual, it is likely to continue to feature as a marker of human civilisation. Not all view the compulsion to repeat as a pathological response. Juda (1983) argues that repetition compulsion is simply a healthy way in which the human condition assimilates new data, a function of the cohesive self. This might explain the response of patients whose experience does not match their expectations, but is a weak argument against the consistently destructive forces evidenced in the world financial markets. This sentiment is illustrated by the following quote from an interviewee who reflects on the future:

> "And gradually you will get back to a position where you will have to incentivise people because the cost of not incentivising them will be greater and you'll go back and say, we had to pay the bonuses."

Here, the inevitability of repetition, of mistakes made and which are likely to continue to be made, is highlighted. The ongoing observation provided me with numerous opportunities for understanding and interpretation, akin to the psychoanalytic encounter where patients relive their experiences in the transference, providing them with the insights that facilitate change (Steiner, 2008). Freud later came to interpret the compulsion to repeat as an expression of resistance to change, of "daemonic power" (Freud, 1920g, p. 21). It can be seen in this way as a resistance to creativity and to life, an anti-life instinct, caught up in a relationship with envy and hatred of anything new (Feldman, 2000; Steiner, 2008).

The longevity of the study provided me with a compulsion to observe and draw on the crisis in a way that a short-term project would have failed to do. I was able to note patterns of behaviour in managing the stress and anxiety of closure and the defences employed to protect those within the system from that stress and anxiety.

The research itself was, in this way, a demonstration of the death drive at work. I was caught up in a compulsion to repeat and the object of my observation became smaller and smaller: individuals disappeared week on week, desk spaces became empty, large office expanses became condensed into a small cluster of desks. Although I was evicted from my position before the final shutdown, I was close to the end, perhaps killed off before the last rites were read.

As I walk into the open-plan space, I immediately sense things are different. Desks normally cluttered with hand cream, mugs, cuddly toys, and cards are now clear. In one bank of desks, I notice the absence of the usual cardigan hanging over the back of a chair. Mike, who was to my left, has moved further down the office. The box of fruit sits at the end of an empty bank of eight desks.

During the period of the observation, physical changes marked the slow crawl of death. Where there had been a large expanse of desks, buzzing with people and artefacts, as the months moved on this space condensed and the personal effects began to disappear. Several people who stayed moved to other desks; every week there was another configuration of sorts. My observation post remained constant, as did the position of the two managers next to me and diagonally opposite my viewing place. No matter how many people were in the department, certain rituals were repeated: the security checks into the building, the fruit box at the end of the bank of each desks, the management meetings, the displays of food, and the call for fun and jokes. These behaviours were repeated again and again, nothing, it appeared, could stop these activities.

There is a link here to Kleinian notions of manic reparation (Klein, 1984b[1940]). We saw in mourning that the destructive impulses we hold can be recognised and a process of reparation can allow the mourning organisation to separate destructive impulses to allow an integration of the good and the bad. This reparation leads to a working through and an acknowledgement of loss. In manic reparation, such obstacles cannot be overcome. In manic reparation, the pain is denied and has to be endlessly repeated. True reparation would entail a separation intolerable to the organisation or individual clinging to the omnipotent control of the organisation, or other object in question. Manic reparation leads to boom and bust, boom and bust.

Aggression and hatred

The death drive gives us a deeper understanding of the aggressive elements of mental life. Freud describes the death instinct as a wish to annihilate the self, to dissolve and return to nothingness. This is akin to aggression, as interpreted by Klein as a projection of an individual's self-destructive drive. Both Freud and Klein place aggression centrally in an analysis of the death drive. Bion's (1961) basic assumption fight/flight (baF) is also relevant here. The aggression expressed a "fight" response to the leaders of the system and perceived perpetrators of the collapse and a "flight" response represented a return to the denial of the drama and tragedy of the collapse. Aggression is, therefore, expressed as a destructive process directed against the self and against others or other objects.

Primal sadism is the Freudian phrase for a part of the death instinct, identical to masochism that remains within the person, partly as a component of the libido and partly with the self as an object. Primal sadism is the function of pure death instinct, while primal, or primary, masochism results from a mixture of libidinal drives and the death instinct (Rycroft, 1995).

Aggression manifested itself in many forms during the slow death of Interbank. The public expressed their anger and fury towards the bank over their loss through demonstrations, public humiliation, and violent acts. Interbank expressed their own aggression towards the senior management, whom they blamed for their deceit and the bank's downfall. Senior management, in turn, directed their anger towards the leaders and the media, whom they saw as causing and inflaming the crisis, respectively. The financial crisis was then blamed by the media on the banking industry as a whole, depicted as corrupt, greedy, and hedonistic. Aggression was self-directed by the employees of Interbank: they derided themselves, they should have seen it coming, they had been fools.

> "Quite honestly, you know, people had bought shares and done incredibly well and had lived a very good lifestyle because it was seen as a very good bet. And over a period of twenty years people did very well out of it. But it collapsed and so, you know, there were a lot of very angry people."

Anger and rage were described by research participants in a variety of ways. The expression of rage from those outside the organisation towards the bank and the industry was a prominent feature. There was a great sense of the injustice of this anger in some, that the fury of the public was misguided and that they were innocents in this fiasco. Another feature of the anger was from inside the organisation towards the media and those they saw as fuelling and stoking the crisis. For some, their greatest fury was directed towards those leaders of the bank whom they saw as executing a massive betrayal, with no apology or explanation. This anger was further fuelled by the lack of account-ability in those deemed to be responsible and their failure to pay for these mistakes. The bitterness that remained was palpable.

The final element of anger was self-directed, with participants angry with themselves for failing to see the writing on the wall and for trusting those whose interests were self-serving.

> "If one objectively looks at it, one would have to say that it is a crooked organisation. Look at what they did, and therefore venom is due."

When the signs are too blatant to ignore, the reality of the demise sinks in; one could say the reality bites. This recognition led to a range of responses, notably aggression and anger directed in a variety of ways as a means of blaming others for the disaster that has befallen the organisation. This anger was expressed towards the organisation by the press and the public, internally towards the leaders, and, on occasion, in a self-destructive manner.

The hated object: Interbank

> "Banks are hated for who they are fundamentally. And some of the public are very perturbed about . . . not perturbed, it's the wrong word for it. Very disgusted with bankers in general."

The bank received many projections of anger and hatred from the outside. The public expressed disgust at the behaviour of Interbank. Public taunts and verbal and physical abuse were reported and discussed. The retreat from public spaces by the bank was expressed most keenly in the headquarters where signage was removed from the outside of buildings, and corporate branding was hidden away. This rebranding was also evident in the City of London, as noted in the following observation in October 2011:

> I notice something different in the first-floor lobby. Signage that says New Interbank—I wonder if this is new or if I have simply not noticed this before.

The stigma of working for Interbank was more profoundly expressed in the headquarters as the City was so identified with the organisation and so many individuals had benefited and suffered from the prolific nature of their lending and borrowing. In the midst of the City of London, Interbank was just another failing bank. In the headquarters, it was the object of utter hatred and disgust.

> "We're not supposed to exist at all. We've had two years during which people protest, protesting outside, marching up and down. Reception used to be on the ground floor on the street; we closed that and moved it up so the whole idea is we don't have any public face wherever possible. There is no public face. . . . It gives employees nothing to identify with."

Individuals within the bank appear truly dismayed that they are the targets of such abuse. They focus on their loss; the organisation that they used to identify with so strongly is now an organisation that cannot even be named. Their place of work, once a location of idealisation and reverie, is now a tainted object, one that does not even deserve to be named in public. The reference to lack of existence extends from the organisation to the individuals themselves. Not all interviewees spoke of personal experiences of abuse and anger, but the comment below is typical. There was a climate of fear surrounding the response to Interbank; people would not name their place of work out of shame and out of fear of attack.

> "I didn't experience it greatly but I know lots of people who really experienced bad things with people, verbally abused and horrible stuff, you know. As if they were the individual responsible for bringing down the entire system rather than you're an employee of an organisation which failed."

Violence, and the threat of violence, pervaded the experience of employees. In the headquarters, visitors from the City of London office were briefed: keep your identity to yourself, do not openly state your destination, describe yourself as an accountant not a banker. Such subterfuge was enacted to protect employees in the headquarters from abuse. Visitors to the headquarters office are told not to say where they are going when they take a taxi from the airport; they should be dropped around the corner, an indication of the presence of fear, shame, and a threat of violence. Such caution could be seen as an overreaction, a dramatic response to the closure of the bank. However, this aggression was not merely in the mind:

> "Bricks being thrown in Interbank offices, and a couple of suicides that the employees had, that has happened. But it's the anger that you can see from the public that is causing all that."

Here, an interviewee goes so far as to blame the public. If they were not so angry, there would not be these violent attacks, perhaps even the suicides could have been prevented. The interviewee does not go on to consider the culpability of those in charge of the bank, but prefers to defend himself from that knowledge and project his own blame on the public.

The sense of disbelief was also expressed. When it dawned that this collapse was real, that the organisation was in downfall, the anger emerged.

> "When it hit the wall we kind of went, is this really happening? And then you get yes it did really happen! And then you get the anger which is, as we all know, you go through and you arrive back, kind of saying well look, that's the new world order, this is where we are at."

Among this climate of fury and uncertainty, there was also very little communication with those who were left trying to run what remained of the bank. There was reference to the media as a source of communication. As dialogue dried up internally, managers turned to the newspapers to find out what was happening to their employer. This contrasts dramatically with the pride in which people spoke of communication in the good years; open dialogue and easy access to senior managers was proudly described.

> "I think [it was] a nightmare scenario from a corporate perspective because every single thing that we knew was being attacked. Three people who were in control were no longer there. So there was no control."

The management of the bank, those that acted as a boundary between the public and the media and the staff, had absconded. Those left to run the ship did so without knowledge and were unable to deal with queries or have their own questions answered. They were in the dark. The influence of the media emerged in a number of interviews and the way in which their sorrow was being played out so publicly.

"Again, that's a lot led by the media and the way the media portrays certain organisations. But what the media don't do is differentiate between trading and banking. You know there is, there's two distinct types of banking. One is commercial lending and one's investment banking/speculating. And you know the commercial side of it is running our country. The investment side was the greed, the corporate greed that not, not 95%, probably more than that, of bankers aren't party to."

The organisation had the experience of being attacked; almost mob behaviour from the public demonstrating a gang state of mind (Canham, 2002). This is different from the gang at work (Stein & Pinto, 2011): here, the public turned in on the institution.

"I just went home and I was boiling, you know, with fury. Because again my integrity was being tested and you sort of get into that sort of personal emotions. And I said to my wife, this is outrageous."

Externalising the disturbing knowledge of the betrayal of revered and respected leaders, as well as the horrific consequences on individual lives of the bank's behaviour, is congruent with projection. This instinctual behaviour, projection, is described by Freud as a means to protect the individual from pain by attributing the cause to external sources. In this way, it is the banking industry that is to blame, or the senior management, or the media who twist and destroy the truth. The cry from the injured and pained is, "It wasn't us, it was them!"

The hated leaders

"... no regard for humankind."

Those left working in the bank directed anger and fury towards the leaders, whom they described as self-serving and inhumane. Their actions disgusted their employees and they provoked an extreme reaction of aggression.

> "I do find the senior management that has been installed on site here a disgrace. Quite personally, quite frankly is that I think they are incredibly self-serving. They have no regard for humankind. No regard whatsoever. They don't treat people well."

Anger towards the senior management, and particularly towards the CEO, who was seen as extremely charismatic, was at times expressed reluctantly. This reluctant anger was expressed almost as if they did not want to believe that he had acted in the way that he had.

> "So people were making decisions that I learnt were inappropriate. And no one is questioning what they've delivered. They have just failed massively. And I think the culture, the dynamic, I think just the lack of desire to understand what had happened, was just extraordinary. Offensive, actually."

The behaviour of the senior management was compounded by their lack of remorse and failure to apologise for what had gone wrong. The love and adoration of the chairman made the failure to deal with the collapse humanely particularly painful for the people who were part of the bank. They had bought into the sense of family and camaraderie and were devastated by the betrayal.

> "People felt very betrayed . . . didn't say sorry. And, you know, if he'd got in there early on saying look I'm really sorry, you know this, everyone was doing it but maybe I shouldn't have, and you know, he possibly could have."

Others were more brutal and expressed a wish for retribution. This fury ran across both sites of the research:

> "I just hope the guys that were responsible for some of the big deals that have been arrested since do actually face, face the consequences of their actions. There was this incredible mix of emotions going on inside the organisation. It was very volatile, I think there are lots of people who are culpable for the reason why we got into this mess and why the world has got into this mess."

It is them not us, we are not bankers like those greedy and immoral workers who caused the crisis is the sentiment that seems to be expressed here. The interviewee here speaks of the difference between the people working at the bank in roles that were remunerated by a standard salary, without the large bonuses and share deals, and those that received those benefits. There seems to be a call for clarity, that they are honest workers, not the dirty workers associated with the greed of the City and the crash. The speaker expresses concern that they have been caught up in a corrupt system, there is blame and distance, the cry is "this is not fair"; the speaker sees himself as a victim in this scenario. There was a strong sense that it was grossly unfair that people were financially rewarded for diabolical behaviour.

> "There was a lot of anger here . . . We've been working so hard here and we've been working and the rest of the bank was doing it."

This interviewee speaks of the anger and frustration; they have been working so hard and look at what the others have been doing. The leaders have let them down and they become the hated and blamed objects.

The hated self

Anger was also self-directed, with echoes of the melancholic self-reproach. This introjected anger was evident to some degree. People described their disappointment in themselves, that they had not seen these troubles coming.

> "No I was angry. I was angry. I was angry at more, first of all at myself, how stupid I was, because my wife at home was telling me, she said you have too many shares, sell, sell them. And I said no, no, this is only a temporary blip thing, they will go up."

The banker was unable to see the truth and colluded with the fantasy. The banker's wife, located outside of the organisation, seemed able to see much more clearly the damaging situation the organisation was in. Viewing the crisis from the outside provided the distance that allowed her to name the reality, to urge her husband to sell. But this was a message that was not heard, could not be heard; if it had been, then all that was held in the organisation would be lost and his faith would have been unfounded. So, when the crash came, this intervie-wee was primarily directing his anger internally.

"But I don't think I will ever lose the bitterness. I have always been on the optimistic side; glass has always been half full."

There is a tone of self-blame in this interviewee, who laments his lost optimistic view of life; bitterness has seeped in and tainted his current and anticipated future experience. Aggression can be mobilised to defend against narcissistic injury. In the case of an organ-isation that views itself as worthy and blameless, this can lead to attacks on the external world for failing to recognise their worth. The fantasy that an organisation must continue to exist, despite facts about poor market position and performance, is a fantasy explored in the notion of the inevitability of organisations (Levine, 2001)

Envy

The death drive is expressed psychically in envy; it is expressed in the desire to take away something desirable that another person possesses (Spillius et al., 2011). Klein sees the death drive as dominating early development and envy as the manifestation of the death drive. She develops Freud's notion of the death drive to encompass envy. In an environment of the City, with colleagues and competitors achieving highly and appearing to continue to relish the financial fortune previ-ously associated with Interbank, envy, the desire to take away and destroy that which belongs to others, can be seen to manifest itself.

Envy is often overlooked in the study of psychoanalysis of organ-isations (Stein, 2000), possibly because of its late arrival in the devel-opment of Kleinian theory (her writing on envy and gratitude was not published until 1957). Envy as a paradigm, separate from anxiety and defences against anxiety, are simultaneously linked and interrelated, including the defences against envy. Envy can be seen to link to aggression: "an oral-sadistic and anal-sadistic expression of sadistic impulses" (Klein, 1957, p. 176). Klein regarded primitive envy as a "direct derivative of the death instinct" (Rosenfeld, 1971, p. 121).

On the societal level, Interbank had appeared to be a bank that was almost perfect; it was successful, loved, nurturing, recognised, innovative, and creative. Its leader was cherished and adored. As CEO, he was "the most charismatic man in the entire world".

The leader here is almost a mystic, a mystic who had been able to create a symbiotic relationship with his followers in the organisation (Bion, 1985), but this symbiotic relationship could not be maintained once the organisation began to crumble and the business failings were exposed. At this point, the relationship becomes more akin to that of a parasitic relationship: both parties are destroyed, the leader falls from his pedestal as mystic, and the followers are crushed in their realisation that their leader has betrayed and misled them. Bion describes this relationship as most akin to envy, where "envy begets envy, and this self-perpetuating emotion finally destroys host and parasite alike" (Bion, 1985, p. 131).

The organisation was described as an ideal, almost intoxicating, place to work. The leader could woo the crowds and the work gave the individuals in the organisation power and a sense of omnipotence.

> "Yeah, and I think that was ... errr ... a tribute equally to the people who were in control that they gave you that kind of power. And the empowerment is amazing ... absolutely amazing."

This was, therefore, an organisation idealised and a leader adored. When the trouble with the bank began, however, the swing to attack was felt forcefully.

> "Verbally abused and horrible stuff, you know. And as if they were the individual responsible for bringing down the entire system, rather than you're an employee of an organisation which failed."

Grenvy, a term coined by Coltart (1989), combines the primal mixture of greed and envious desire, split into greedy desire and malign envy of objects willing, but unable, to help. From profound feelings of helplessness, envy develops as a defence, leading to idealisation and denigration. This is a useful term to apply to the organisation before its downfall.

Pairing of leader and researcher

The presence of a researcher in the midst of the collapsing organisa-tion was also a reminder of my separation from the organisation. Without an outsider, those who are part of the system can imagine themselves to be at one, in primal unity with the organisation. The death of the organisation is experienced as a part of themselves dying. An outsider placed in the organisation, with the promise of life outside the organisation, could ignite fierce envy against the inter-loper. Envy was also experienced in the apparent pairing of the leader of the department, Anna, and me as researcher. My visits were always given the impression of being wanted and I was received with warm welcome, with invitations to regular management meetings and to accompany overseas trips extended. I was essentially offered a red carpet to the heart of the organisation. This was my experience of the way in which the research was welcomed by Anna. Her affection for me was evident in her introduction to visitors of me as "her friend" who was doing research.

Such a presentation of a close relationship invited projections of envy and aggression from the team, feelings which ultimately led to my eviction from the role of researcher and a disruption of the pair-ing. Evocative of basic assumption pairing (baP) (Bion, 1961), this primal attack can be understood. The eviction of the researcher was a powerful illustration of negative and silent transference and the asso-ciated destructive impulses (Rosenfeld, 1971). Klein observed, in her work with young children and play, a dualistic urge to destroy their objects and a desire to preserve them (1958). In this research, there was a member, the deputy leader (Elaine), with a strong urge to destroy the research, and a leader (Anna), desperate to preserve the research. The deputy leader, mobilising the death instinct and experiencing anxiety over fear of annihilation, turns the aggression on the persecu-tory object, in this case the researcher (me).

Killing off the researcher

During the eighteenth month of the research, I attempted to organise another visit to the bank after I returned from holiday. In response to my email, I received the following reply from Anna: "The morale has dipped to such an appalling level that I wonder if it might be best to forgo coming into the office at the moment."

I responded to say that I understood and would wait for her to tell me when I could visit again. However, there were no other visits to the department to observe; Anna said it would be best for me to stop coming in at the moment. There was just one final meeting that I requested and was able to organise to express my thanks and bid the team farewell.

When I did meet up with Anna again for an informal lunch, there was a different explanation as to why the visits to the department should be curtailed. The deputy head of department had complained to Human Resources about my presence and my visits were deemed to be unsuitable. I did not get to know the details of the complaint; however, the action "killed off" the research role. In this act, which I interpreted as an envious attack, my life as researcher in the organisation came to an end. This individual mobilised, perhaps on behalf of the system, an attack on an outside object perceived to be thriving and benefiting from the suffering of the team. Here, the death drive manifested itself as envy, as a desire to take away the desirable role that I, as the researcher, possessed. My ability to come and go as I pleased, to be part of the system, yet offering nothing tangible to the work of the team, to have the status of researcher and the prospect of work beyond the dying organisation can be seen to have evoked strong antagonistic and envious feelings.

Contemptuous feelings towards me as a researcher led to a triumphant eviction. My ability to walk away from the destruction of the organisation, even to benefit from it, might have generated lustful feelings towards me and my role. Longing to be on the outside, rather than in the midst of the destruction, led to feelings of envy directed towards my role as researcher, the object of envy.

Summary

This chapter has explored the death drive and drawn on the data gathered to explore the insights of Thanatos to understand organisational closure. It has described the death drive as a return to an earlier inorganic state; it is also associated with violence, with a wish to cancel and to destroy. The chapter explains how the death drive, in all its vicissitudes, operates in the closure of Interbank. It compared the application of the death drive in the City of London with that in the international headquarters. The different expressions of the death drive, of dissolution and destruction, were contrasted.

The chapter examined how the death drive is expressed psychically in envy in the desire to take away something desirable that another person possesses: this was illustrated with vignettes describing the destruction of the leader's car and through the killing off of the researcher. In the competitive environment of the City, envy, the desire to take away and destroy that which belongs to others, was seen to manifest itself (Klein, 1957). The compulsion to repeat mistakes in the world of finance and the cycle of boom and bust that epitomises the City of London was emphasised.

The violence associated with the destructive elements of the death drive was apparent, particularly expressed in the bank's headquarters. It is important to stress that, while this aggression might have manifested itself externally in the organisation's international headquarters, with marches, fire, and public outcries—anger was also experienced in the City of London. Defences were employed to mask this rage, yet it did also emerge.

Death is not just an event approaching through time, but something that is at work in every psychic pore (Eigen, 1995). The poetic and heuristic power of the death drive is striking; we can see how people cling to suffering, a desire, even a full flight, towards death (Eigen, 1995, 2004)

Eros and Thanatos can express themselves in the behaviour of both leaders and others in an organisation. At a vulnerable time of loss, particularly when the organisation had been thought of as vibrant, even immortal, so much more so. We saw, in the expression of mourning and melancholia, the pain of losing the loved object. With Thanatos, hateful and aggressive feelings are given expression. Where the leader was idealised and loved in the melancholic organisation, in the world of Thanatos the leader is destroyed. Aggression and envy is mobilised by the death drive and this has been illustrated. The compulsion to repeat, envy, aggression, and hatred—this is the death drive at work.

CHAPTER SEVEN

Defences at work

F reud introduced the unconscious as a dynamic force, where unconscious phenomena are always trying to make themselves heard and felt (Freud, 1900a; Frosh, 2012). It is defence mechanisms that prevent the unconscious from appearing at all times; these mechanisms protect the individual from disturbing ideas entering conscious awareness. Defence mechanisms are also employed at an organisational level: repression is a useful tool to deny a crisis, projection can be directed to place failure into other, less achieving, organisations, and splitting can be used as a means of protecting the organisation from its less savoury aspects.

The vulnerability of this dying organisation generated profound defensive reactions from those within the institution. These defences were constructed in response to the unbearable anxiety of contemplating insecurity and their uncertain future. Defensive behaviour as a means of protecting oneself from anxieties that are too terrible to bear manifested itself in a variety of guises that are explored during this chapter.

Klein's notion of individual mania (1984a,b) is founded on the principle that "mania is based on the mechanism of denial" (Klein, 1984b, p. 277). It features denial at its foundation, but also omnipo-

tence, triumphalism, and over-activity. Klein's (1959) notions of introjection, projection, and identification are also helpful here. The organisation is internalised and taken into a member of that organisation,
so that the experience of the organisation is not only the external
encounters, but also an internalised experience and being. The organisation is part of that employee. In this way, organisational death is
catastrophic and hard to bear, so defences against the pain of that loss
are employed.

The inability to contemplate mortality has resonance with organisations imbued with a strong attachment and identification with their
host organisation. That the organisation will cease to be is something
that is simply impossible to imagine. Loyalty to, and belief in, the
unique and enduring contribution of the institution dominate employees' thinking. Despite evidence of organisations and markets collapsing around them, individuals cling to the belief that "we will survive".

Coping responses of the teams are, therefore, interpreted as a variety of defence mechanisms. The regular feasts and banquets to celebrate every occasion are interpreted as a manic denial of the inevitable
end, the jolliness and joviality of the team members and the head of
department as a means to manage the pain of the closure. Regular
meetings, procedures, structure, and tight management control of
timekeeping, sick leave, and holiday habits were evident. The demise
of the organisation did not result in a letting up of practice and procedures; on the contrary, at every management meeting I observed, team
leaders were asked to update on the processes established. I saw these
measures function as a means to contain the anxiety of the ending and
a mechanism to make the work bearable through denial.

I observed feasting on a steady stream of sugar-laden snacks, cere-
moniously laid out as a comfort for the sorrows of the day. Extreme
commitment to procedures and policy making at a time when the
organisation had only a short time to live was evidenced. Constant
jokes and hilarity and demonstrations of the place of work as great fun
to be part of were a regular feature. Defence mechanisms, therefore,
blocked a perceived threat by pushing uncomfortable or dangerous
thoughts out of mind. The force of a defence mechanism, be it repression, splitting, or denial, makes it hard to move forward. Energy is
expended in defence, which is illustrated in comparing the response
of the mournful organisation that can work through its anxieties and
the melancholic organisation that is unable to separate from these

anxieties and becomes stuck. Repression causes anxiety; therefore, more repression is needed to deal with that anxiety (Freud, 1926d).

Mania

Mania is an extreme state of mind, one where normal, thoughtful, and considered responses to situations are exaggerated and lead to over-activity. This over-activity protects the individual from feeling vulnerable, with literally no space to think and to consider the possibility of things going wrong. Freud describes mania as similar in content to melancholia, but that in melancholia the ego succumbs to the condition and in mania the condition is pushed to one side.

> But here once again, it will be well to call a halt and to postpone any further explanation of mania . . . As we already know, the interdependence of the complicated problems of the mind forces us to break off every enquiry before it is completed—till the outcome of some other enquiry can come to is assistance. (Freud, 1917e, p. 259)

Klein's characterisation of mania as a sense of omnipotence has particular resonance with Interbank. Individuals within the bank retained the feeling that they were all-powerful and struggled to acknowledge the end. Their rhetoric that continued to promise continued share price rises, market development, and property price inflation suggested they felt themselves superior to the market and to all the evidence of its collapse. This superiority is also reflected in Klein's description of the triumphalism associated with the manic individual (1984b[1940]). Mania and denial are inextricably linked. The lack of thinking in mania leads to denial and an inability to face painful or stressful situations, resulting in the refusal of an idea to move to consciousness: for example, to accept that the closure of the organisation will happen, that the leader of the organisation was corrupt, that the promises of return to glory and financial success were lies.

Denial

"There is a strange thing goes on inside a bubble. It's hard to describe. People who are in it can't see outside of it, don't believe there is an outside" (Prebble, 2009).

The notion of a bubble is a useful way to look at the concept of denial. In the cocoon of the organisation, it is possible to remain focused inwards and to fail to turn around and see the chaos ensuing outside the bubble. An individual may repudiate, unconsciously, all or some of the meaning of an event (Frosh, 2012; Moore & Fine, 1990).

The concept of denial operating in a melancholic organisation differs from the operation of denial in a mourning organisation. Denial in a melancholic sense suggests that problems and difficulties are observed, noted, and responded to, but not in such a way that protects the individual. Interbank was used to its position as market leader, its reified spot in the financial community was accompanied by a sense of superiority, the organisation was good, knew it was good, and could not contemplate being anything other than that. This is one of the reasons why the news of its downfall was so hard to absorb and so painful.

Respondents described the organisation going into free fall or, as described earlier, as if one were falling off a cliff. The environment was experienced as out of control, with no knowledge or communication and a lack of confidence in the leadership team, who appeared in equal turmoil or absent. A minority took pleasure in the chaos. Most struggled with their feelings of being lost, being driven mad, and the difficulty of the uproar and chaos. The inability to see what was before their eyes is illustrated keenly by the observation vignette below. There is evidence of both denial and a manic response to cope with the anxiety and stress of the closure through the application of meeting agendas, procedures, and forced jollity. I quote from an observation held at the beginning of 2012. At this time, contract staff had been notified of the ending of their contracts and were due to leave in two months' time, the name of the organisation had been changed, and the ending appeared in sight. This particular management meeting was exceptionally jolly and light-hearted. I was struck by the juxtaposition of this jolly, self-congratulatory management team—rejoicing in the sunshine activities in their team—with our location in a glass-walled meeting room adjacent to the carnage of a dismantled, chaotic office floor, devoid of life and substance.

The meeting is held on the third floor. We take the lift and enter the floor, which is in a state of carnage—partitions are piled up, furniture is in various stages of being dismantled, carpet squares are piled up in small

mounds, and debris is scattered around the floor. There is a decon-
struction of the open-plan office space in an advanced stage. We walk
across the debris to meeting room 3, one of the glass-walled meeting
rooms around the perimeter of the floor in the far right-hand corner.
No one makes any comment about, or reference to, the state of the
floor. Anna says it is a shame that they will be losing this floor, as they
need the meeting rooms. They are going to lease this floor, she says, I
think to me, to make some money. Anna starts the meeting by saying
"Let's crack on: 'sunshine, showers, rain'—who wants to go first?"

So, what can this business as usual, even business jollier than
usual, activity suggest about the workings of this team? Elements of
mania were evident throughout the period of observation with excessive celebrations with food, "mad" parties, loud jokes, and jesting.

The evasion of grief is a feature of mania and melancholia. One
could argue that their manic jolliness is a defence mechanism against
the trauma played out in the most visual sense before their eyes. One
could further suggest that the jolliest of all players, the head of the
department, was overwhelmed by the need to keep the team "up"
and, therefore, played out the happiest and wittiest of roles to defend
both the team and herself from the vicissitude of her own leadership
role and the roles of her team members. This manic, or pathological,
reparation is based on denial of depressive feelings, or, in the case of
the leader, a compulsion to eliminate depressive anxiety. This contrasts with normal creative reparation, which comes from the depressive position and builds on the wish to restore or repair the damaged
object with love and respect for the object (Klein, 1946).

> "No, don't worry, you know it's . . . we'll weather the storm, it
> will all be fine."

In the face of all the evidence, the resignation of senior management, the appointment of the government to crisis manage the closure,
there was still a sense that this was a blip, something that could be
overcome. The notion of the crisis being temporary occurred again and
again. This description of the catastrophic situation in such light and
temporary terms is illustrative of the depth of denial in operation.

> "The messages internally were very upbeat. You know, don't
> worry about this, it's a funding issue, but that will be addressed.

We will deal with the funding issue, we . . . we are way better than all the other banks. The bad debt issue—not a case. This, we have been hearing about this property bubble for ten years. It hasn't come to pass, it's not going to come to pass, there's huge interest out there. We're great, bank's great. This is just a temporary blip, don't worry about it."

The notion of projective identification (Klein, 1946) also applied. In projective identification, the parts of the self that are unwelcome are split off and projected into external objects. These external objects then become identified with the unwanted parts of the self. For Interbank, this meant projecting into other banks the responsibility and failure: the failure exists in them, not in us; therefore, we will get over this.

"Listen, it's temporary because all the other banks are going down. They will all come back at the same time. So it's not like Interbank was an outlier. All the other financial shares were going down all over the world, it wasn't just [here]. So that kind of said right, well, yeah, we'll ride with it."

There was an element of delusion apparent in the interview data in relation to the leadership of the bank. This applied also to the integrity of the leadership team, a sense that they would not have intentionally deceived them; they must have thought they were acting for the good. There was also a sense expressed that, despite the obvious signs within the bank, the industry, and the world, they would survive and continue to thrive. The feeling expressed was that this crisis was merely a blip in their trajectory.

"And even then, even with everything else going on in the world, it's like oh no, we'll be fine. We will always . . . the share price is always strong, you know. We, we would survive."

"So people were always amazed that, in terms of the commitment and loyalty, and we managed to hold on to it even through the bad times."

The sense of unthought known (Bollas, 1987) also filtered through.

"There were different signals out there that probably we weren't picking up on. Or we were burying our head in the sand a lot."

Later, on reflection, some were able to see that they had been naïve and blind. It is still reticent, however; the respondent swings between the suggestion that probably something was missed, the more blatant denial of literally burying their heads in the sands.

> "Yeah, it made sense. We didn't question it. And . . . but when you look back, and in hindsight it's wonderful, you look back and say right, well the capital markets have frozen up, it's only a matter of time where the funding you have in place is going to run out. And then if liquidity becomes a problem, then prices are going to drop, so the value of collateral is going to suffer. It all made absolute sense but listen, hindsight is wonderful."

Others commented on the denial they witnessed in others. This interviewee links the position of the bank to the global financial crisis, but seems to be a lone voice. His warning is not one that is listened to or heeded.

> "I remember walking into a meeting one day and going: Iceland's just going bankrupt; I just read it on Reuters. And they're kind of going: what do you mean Iceland's gone bankrupt and I was saying Iceland has just gone bankrupt, and that's a fact. And . . . and I was like, no this is just not going and you, you still kind of think, well we can always get out of this."

The pain of confronting the end was very hard to absorb, and the period of denial and mania made the force of the closure hit very hard.

> "But, you know, when certain things have happened to them or they've been given certain pieces of information, it's been something of a shock. And then, you know, the whole department goes 'well I never knew that was going to happen!' Well, you know, we might say why not. This is as plain as the nose on your face, you know. But it's just that nobody gets them to think like that. So, collectively, you have a lot of people who are, you know, don't really have time to adjust to information and it . . . and it just hits them."

That the experience of Interbank was reflective of a crisis beyond the organisation, country, and the globe was expressed by some,

perhaps in seeking meaning for the messy situation they found themselves in, described as "A bad alignment of the planets." The bad
alignment of the planets is blamed here for the financial crisis. There
is denial of individual and organisational responsibility. There is
nowhere on earth to project the blame; the only place to direct the pain
is to the stars.

> "There's a strange sort of emotional bond a lot of the employees
> have with it. Still do, even though they have taken so many blows
> on the way down, you know. And it's, you know, I can't . . . I can't
> fathom it. Because normally you . . . you . . . you feel good about
> an organisation if it's successful, if it's good, if it does its business
> in the right way. You know, you can puff your chest out, you are
> well regarded, you know, it's all that kind of stuff . . . But there is
> still this . . . this strange cohesion. And even as things started to
> fracture . . ."

The interviewee recognises the resistance to let go of the idealised
organisation. There is a puzzle for her: why should there still be such
loyalty and commitment when there has been such betrayal and frac-
ture? This question is answered in part by the mania and denial in
operation. At a conscious level, it was too much for the employees to
take on, so these defences protected them from harsh and painful
truths.

Greed

> "Life is long enough, and a sufficiently generous amount has been
> given to us for the highest achievements if it were all well invested."
>
> (Seneca, 1997: I)

The notion of greed, of a dissatisfaction with our lot suggests that for
greed, all of nature is too little. That for those who desire more and
more there will always be a sense of desire, of not being satisfied with
one's lot.

Seneca implies that it is impossible to sate desire and to be content
with your lot. Psychoanalysis is more interested in the way in which

desire drives greed. Psychoanalytically greed is rooted in its origins in infancy. For Klein (1946, 1952), the infant's greed is linked to introjection and the desire to bring the objects into the self. To incorporate the bad objects, the infant is fulfilling a phantasy that this is a way in which the object can be destroyed. These concepts are related to the paranoid–schizoid position, where a splitting process occurs between the good and the bad object, the good and the bad breast, one a force of destruction, the other a source of food and satisfaction. The bad breast is associated with aggressive instincts from a persecutory breast, a part-object; good feelings are seen as coming from the loving and giving breast. Klein sees these urges as both creative and destructive, both life giving and death seeking, and both creative and destructive. The infant might feed greedily until the supply is drained, perhaps in fear that there will be no more.

Greed can be understood as a wish to take in as many good objects as possible, to alleviate the damaged objects inside (Klein, 1957). The context of the research, in the City in an environment reeling from the effects of voracity and fantasy about the ongoing and unending rise of the markets, greed could be described as being at home (*Heimlich*— there is nothing uncanny about it). The financial climate prior to the 2008 collapse was sympathetic to Gordon Gekko, a character in Oliver Stone's 1987 film *Wall Street*, his iconic words, *greed is good*, rang true. Greed as a factor in the collapse of the City in 2008, fuelled by blind ambition, and distance from the risk of lending through products such as credit derivatives, featured in an assessment of the collapse (Tett, 2009). Such a relationship with greed and excess was witnessed during the research.

The excess of unending credit, ongoing success, and gilded status was beguiling and infectious. This environment of financial greed was crushed by the collapse, but greed continued to manifest itself in other forms. Food, celebration, and feasting were consistently evidenced during the eighteen-month observation. There were displays of largely sweet and snack food set up at different stations throughout the department, virtually every week of my research.

The following vignette from an observation is an example:

> To the right is a desk at the end covered with snacks and food. Two tubes of Smarties, a tube of milk chocolate white buttons, a tin of chocolate biscuits, a tin of Quality Street, a bag of cookies, and a bag of chocolate.

> The women on either side of this spread get up three or four times during the observation to examine the items and collect small handfuls of carefully selected goods. The selection process could take up to five minutes, with discussion and menus of chocolates consulted. A woman is in front of the "feast" table, she makes her selection of goods.

This observation demonstrates the use of food to comfort and indulge, but also to distract. The numerous visits to the food table offered a chance to think of things other than work, or the future of that work. The abundance of the food is also illustrative; it is not a biscuit offered with a cup of tea, but a full table of food stuffs that might be categorised as treats. There is also the repetition of visits to the table; the consumption had no end, as long as it was there, people returned again and again to feed and feast. On another week, there is a more noisy encounter with the food:

> There is a fair amount of noise at this time, and movement around the office. At one end of the bank of desks there is a large selection of food—flavoured crisps, cakes, biscuits, jam tarts, doughnuts. Across the office there is a red balloon with "Birthday princess" printed on it tied to someone's chair. Another woman spends very little time at her desk and gets up and down, to get food, to speak to someone, to get a mint from a colleague. She makes loud comments. When she gets up from her desk, others come over to talk to colleagues and borrow her chair—she returns and says loudly, "If anyone takes my chair again I'm going to resign"; this has happened four times, she says. She is constantly getting food and snacks and appears to spend very little time engaged in work.

The atmosphere of this environment is informal and celebratory. The range of snacks is bite sized and sugar or salt laden, colourful and artificial. Each item seems to be offering an immediate salve or satisfaction for a craving. The food again creates movement and focus, an appealing focus away from computer terminals and paperwork. The manic interaction of the employee woman with the food is illustrative of this up and down, unsettled atmosphere. Her reference to resignation is bizarre; she will resign if anyone takes her chair, yet she is not working. Her chair is there as a symbol of her place in the organisation which, like the organisation, she expects to be there when she has had her fill, but she is up and down.

A box of fruit appears as symbolic of a more moderate and even approach to consumption; it sits forlornly at the end of the bank of desks, untouched in competition with the sweet and sugary snacks. The fruit boxes are a corporate initiative that encourages the consumption of more fruit among employees. It seems to speak of moderation in competition with excess, the appeal of an apple or banana against the delights of a tray of sweet cakes or chocolates. Even as the desks emptied of their occupants, this box of fruit remained, a symbol of healthier times for the business. However, it also symbolises the choice of this organisation and the choices of the City of London. Moderation and sensible consumption was possible, yet this path was side-lined for the giddy and gluttonous alternative.

Over the course of the observation, it seemed there were occasions to celebrate almost every week. Diwali, International Food Day, Chinese New Year, birthdays, exam success, welcomes and departures, consolation over a romantic break-up, engagements, graduations, bake days, cake competition days, and so on. The numerous occasions seemed an almost frantic effort to create a comforting and enjoyable environment. They provided another opportunity for celebration, not to be missed. No time for work.

Weight control and the discussion of diets were directed most vocally to one normally proportioned man in his twenties who accepted the jibes about his weight and how he would look in a pair of Speedos. He often referred to the diet he was going to start and others referred to it, too. This categorisation of James as the "fat one" was interesting, as there were a number of women around him who could have been described as obese and certainly appeared a great deal fatter than this normal-looking man. He was willing to be the container on which greed and gorging was projected; his normality perhaps gave him the strength to bear these projections.

The appetite for food extended to cake competitions; entries are discussed and rated. One in particular is an iced celebration cake.

There is a cake as part of a master chef-style competition discussed. Anna shows me a picture of an iced cake that reads: FAREWELL INTERBANK. Judging will take place later in the day, she tells me.

Who is the winner (and the loser) of the competition that celebrates the ending of their work at the bank? It is a curious presentation of ways to satisfy their appetite for distraction. Lunch is described by Altman and Baruch (2010) as a chance to construct a *liberated* personal and team identity. Interestingly, lunch was rarely a shared office experience and appeared to be something consumed outside of the office; the exodus at key points of the day, 12.30 p.m. and 5.00 p.m., were noticeable and military. Anna used these lunch breaks as a time to internet shop and "be free in the office space". She described her purchases and bargains, the discounts she managed to secure.

Shoes lined the space next to her desk; more shoes and boots, bags, coats, and fashion items were regularly described.

> I walk to my desk and see that Elaine and Anna have just returned to their desks. We greet each other and Anna immediately tells me she must show me her new boots. She opens the Top Shop website and shows me a pair of platform, over the knee, high-heeled black boots. Alongside her desk is a display of high-heeled shoes in a variety of colours, lined up.

Food was not the only way in which greed was manifest; I examine now the corporate branded goods that were a feature of the observation and my own greed and gorging as researcher.

Corporate goodies (tainted goods)

The taint of working in an institution that has been deemed to be greedy, reckless, and wildly irresponsible is perhaps deepened by the knowledge that, unlike other institutions that appeared to function in a similar way, this institution is destined to death whereas others have been saved. The negative ethical and social connotations of such financial dirty work have stigmatised the work that once brought the employees enormous pride and hope for the future. This is particularly evident in the home base of this organisation.

> I am sitting in my usual observation position and today I am engaged in conversation a few times. There is a pile of products at the far end of the office. People are walking around with canvas bags, stationery, and also leather portfolio cases. There is traffic to and from the end of the office with people carrying little piles of corporate goods back to their desks. Anna shows me a leather portfolio case and asks if I would I like one. I am torn, but say yes, I would like one. She walks down to the end of the office and returns with a black leather zipped portfolio case and

an electronic ruler. This, she says, is for you. It is embossed with the bank's name on the front cover of the portfolio case. She then takes out a box (a box she has shown me before) that contains a corporate gift, a branded silver harmonica. She holds the box up and asks me what I might imagine is in there? She then reveals the harmonica and CD instructions, she points out the sticker on the harmonica (as she did last time), and I smile. She then goes through the same routine with Rachel. Dan, who sits to my left, offers me a cap that is on his desk, I say thank you but no, I have the portfolio case. People are wandering around the office with piles of canvas bags, caps, and stationery but only one portfolio case each.

There is a gorging on these free gifts that causes a ripple of excitement through the office. I learn subsequently that these corporate goodies could not be seen in public in the home city of this organisation, such was the anger, resentment, and vitriol directed towards the institution. Those working at a distance, in the satellite in the City of London, cushioned by other financial institutions struggling in a similar vein, faced less of a stigma and were able to accept these gifts apparently without this taint. These "perks" could, therefore, be liberally shared with the London staff, who were unaware of the distasteful response their exposure would elicit elsewhere. This pile of treats was also a collection of symbolic debris—artefacts that represented the good times and the pride in, and the aspirational essence of, this organisation.

The contrast of the two sites of the research is illustrated by the response to these corporate goodies (for the City of London) and tainted goods for the HQ office. In the latter, people described public demonstrations and marches against the bank that led employees to fear revealing their place of work. This is illustrated by the sharing of the corporate goods in the City of London office, as a bonus, whereas in the HQ, people would be fearful of carrying any object that bore the company logo.

This regular feasting and gorging reflected the greed and indulgence of the City and of the banking industry, an embodiment of the fat cat bankers.

Researcher's greed and gorging

During the eighteen months of observation, I did not eat any of the food or taste any of the dishes brought to work. I was offered snacks, sweets, and chocolates on a number of occasions, largely early on in the observation, but this is something I resisted. However, my own greed in role was reflected in my devouring of information and observation. I did not offer any interpretations to the organisation or to the management team. I was merely the observer and the recipient of information and experience. Therefore, this one-way relationship offered no palpable containment of the anxiety experienced in the closure. Unconscious associations of an outsider caring enough to observe were, none the less, relevant. Yet, perhaps there was concern about my appropriate use of the data I gathered. The following observation at a management meeting suggests so.

> Before the meeting starts, BJ talks about how itchy his moustache is (he has told me previously he is growing the moustache to raise money for research into prostate cancer). He says he just hopes that the funds raised are appropriated in the right way.

He directs these comments to me: is this some coded message about what I will do with the data I have collected? Will I be using the data appropriately? Or, possibly, this is a reference to the inappropriate use of funds by the bank. More will be said about this in Chapter Eight.

Splitting

The research uncovered a range of polar descriptions—those who were tarnished, and those untarnished, those who were employable, and those who would never get a job again, those who had been honourable and honest, and those who had been dishonourable and deceitful. There was a great deal of data supporting the notion of the idealised organisation and the idealised leadership. Destructive and dishonest behaviour was split off from the organisation into other corporations, the economy, and the broader society. There was an inability to integrate the organisation and its leadership, the good and the bad; it remained a much loved entity with hate and disgust being directed outside the organisation.

> "And so when the downturn came, the failings of Interbank were exposed very starkly, and, you know, the horrible statistic is that

at one point it was the most successful bank in the world in terms of return on capital and then it was the least successful bank in the world."

The polarisation of the organisation, perceived by the participants pre-crash as magnificent, the most successful institution of its kind, contrasted with its portrayal by those outside and in the media as the worst of institutions, greedy, badly run, and irresponsible. The leader was equally described as a god and a demon.

"Now we were just being hammered. You just give up reading newspapers. There were headlines every day. Every day . . . there was something every day."

The bank had swung dramatically from one end of the spectrum of public opinion to the other. It moved from being the most loved institution, a place held for a number of years, to the most hated over a short time frame. Its fall from grace was compounded by the public nature of the collapse and the constant press coverage and speculation. This speculation was something those inside the organisation identified with; they, too, were unaware of the way in which the organisation could have failed so spectacularly.

"I ended up in a very interesting slot. I would say, you know, literally at the heart of the most hated financial institution."

Being the object of hatred with the media and the community was described as interesting. Yet, such an experience, particularly in contrast to the "high" of working in the organisation that was so loved and admired cannot but have been catastrophic.

"And it suddenly got worse. We had the ignominy of being the largest ever corporate loss in history, the largest ever bank loss, the worst performing bank from the top performing bank, which is horrible. You were seeing . . . it's still in the papers, you couldn't get away from it. And, of course, everybody knew who you were."

The organisation was presented as an object of hate and derision. It was described by interviewees as being blamed for the world's financial crisis, the scapegoat for all that had gone wrong with the world's financial performance. The data also linked to the broader network of bankers, identifying themselves with other bankers who had also been blamed for the financial crisis. For some interviewees, this was justified, for others, there was a defensive response with counter-attack on other bodies of responsibility, such as the government.

> "So it's been a remarkable journey. I mean in the last three years; it's been difficult but prior to that times were very, very different. You were in a really flying organisation. It was quoted a million times as the best bank in the world, you name it. And so you went from that accolade to hell's fire and damnation, almost with the time. That and the loss of . . . getting accustomed to an altering mind-set."

The splitting of the developing ego into good and bad objects is relevant for Klein and others in the object relations school. However, at the root of this splitting are the unconscious processes Freud identified. The splitting process is not conscious, but is driven by unknown feeling and desire. In incorporating the "bad" object, the infant is left with greater hunger for "good" objects; in this way, the good object becomes persecutory. The urge to fill the inner void, the greed, is the desperate attempt of the infant to avoid hunger. In paranoid–schizoid thinking, there is an urge to overwhelm persecutory objects with good objects. The violence of their incorporation means they can turn immediately persecutory. In the depressive mode, there is, in contrast, a motivation to repair good objects.

Splitting can be directed internally and externally, to other individuals and to organisations. Splitting is, therefore, a defence mechanism, but can also represent a normal and constructive part of our mental functioning. Splitting allows us to separate unbearable feelings of anxiety. In a depressive position, the individual is able to hold both good and bad, offering some reparation, but, in paranoid–schizoid thinking, intolerable feelings overwhelm, they can be cut off and separated by a process of splitting. In melancholia, however, this latter application of splitting is applied. In Kleinian terms, the unpalatable, destructive, and "bad" part of the crisis was split off from the strong, energetic, and life-giving organisation of which they were part. Literally, there was always somebody else to blame.

"There was always somebody else to blame for it, which I think, you know, in some ways when you've worked for an organisation like that and the leadership was so strong and directive and everybody believed the story, for it to have collapsed was just like literally an extraordinary tale. People could not quite get their heads [round it] or comprehend what was happening."

This separation of good and bad was extended to the organisation and to the leader, featuring a strong idealisation of the leader.

"I think we all knew that the emperor wasn't wearing a coat but we didn't know that he was naked! And so when the downturn came, the failings of Interbank were exposed very starkly, and . . . and, you know, the horrible statistic is that at one point it was the most successful bank in the world in terms of return on capital, then it was the least successful bank in the world."

Idealisation of the organisation and the leader persisted in the narrative of the interviewees. In the face of their experiences and their tales of loss and betrayal, participants continued to muse about the positive features of the organisation, the way it empowered and rewarded people and the atmosphere of friendliness and energy. Interviewees assumed I was in the "know", that I was aware of the loyalty and love felt for the organisation:

"I will have good memories of it and everything. You've probably heard this from a lot of people; we used to say if you cut yourself, you bleed Interbank colours . . . because people were just so committed to the organisation, myself included, and people saw themselves making their career here, staying. Like, most people move around every couple of years, but people were very . . . committed to staying, and . . . ummm . . . and making, you know, being there for, you know, this great company."

There was tremendous vanity in the way things were done. Their practice and the business model were great sources of pride for people working in the bank. That this model and practice led to corruption, deceit, and downfall was not acknowledged.

Splitting was also expressed in love and hate of the leader. The leader was similarly presented as a man of integrity and energy, someone who took care to take an interest in all the people working for the bank, not just the senior people. He was seen as someone who was hard working, charismatic, and successful.

> "Jack was hugely charismatic. And I mean he was charismatic in all walks of life. I mean, you could see the way he'd get on outside of work. He was a man about town, you know."

The balance of data shared was weighted very much towards love and idealisation of the leader. Splitting off the unbearable part of oneself or one's experience and placing those difficult to face issues in another being or object was evidenced. Others were greedy, unrealistic, and uncommunicative, but it was impossible to see those characteristics in themselves.

Splitting was evident in the way in which the organisation was viewed and the way in which the leadership was loved and hated. This was not in equal measure: the glow of success and achievement clung to the Interbank employees and it was hard for them to acknowledge the mess they were in.

> "He was a complete hate figure, he went from absolutely everyone loves him to, to a complete hate figure, which I don't think he actually deserves. I do agree there are people out there who have done more or less the same."

Even when expressing the hatred towards the leader, there was some justification for what he had done, almost as if they did not want him to receive the hatred. The hatred was largely placed outside of them; it was a reference to "they" who hate him, rather than "I". The shock of his vilification and disbelief in it seemed still to resonate:

> "That was part of dynamic change in the bank and then, from that point really, the bank was just going at a phenomenal rate. Profits were going at 30%. He was voted businessman of the year, year after year after year. Now they absolutely detest him."

There were numerous plaudits for Jack, still adored after all they had been through; it seemed that it was too painful to acknowledge his flaws, so he remained idealised in their eyes despite the desperate situation they found themselves in.

Summary

The inability to integrate the good and the punishing/destructive sides of the bank was impossible. Individuals were unable to cope with the loss of the organisation and became inward looking, losing interest in the outside world. The chapter showed how defences against the death of the organisation were evidenced and presented in emergent themes of mania, denial, greed, and splitting. Klein's theory has been helpful (1952, 1957) in building on the original contribution of Freud. She helps us to understand the primitive roots that lie behind the behaviour that tends to idealise some object or person and to demonise another. Klein's work suggests that the wish by some to perpetuate a caring society (or organisation) is an expression of a wish to introject the caring and maternal institutions, alongside paternal authority, leading to integration, concern, and reparation (Minsky, 1996).

The chapter has examined the defended response of individuals, vulnerable within this dying organisation. At times, these were profound. They were defences that were constructed in response to the unbearable anxiety of their loss, their uncertainty about the future, and their insecurity. Defensive behaviour as a means of protecting oneself from anxieties that are too terrible to bear manifested itself in a variety of guises examined here. In this organisation, those defences were demonstrated in mania and denial and in greed and splitting.

CHAPTER EIGHT

Ending thoughts

D eath is a subject that absorbs, provokes, and fascinates. Mortal death and organisational death share a great deal: both involve loss and change, both can be painful, and both can elicit mourning and melancholia. There is no one who has experienced death, but the experience of death surrounds us, as does the death drive that exists at work as well as in our psyche.

This work has provided an intimate bedside portrait of an organisation in a palliative state. I have brought the concept of the death drive and Freud's work on "Mourning and melancholia" (1917e) and the death drive (1920g, 1930a) into the workplace and used this important stream of psychoanalytic thought as a means of interrogating and further understanding organisational life, developing an analysis of mourning and melancholia in an organisation and bringing the subject of death at work to the surface.

As a result of this investigation, I found that mourning is applicable to organisational loss; there was evidence of employees working through organisational death. Chapter Four identified the ways in which employees dealt with the organisational collapse in a manner consistent with mourning and one which could be described as "normal". That is, pain and distress were evidenced, but this was experienced as a stage and a response that could then be processed and an alternative future of work contemplated and accepted. These employees were able to operate in a sophisticated work mode (Bion, 1961) and were able to reach a depressive position (Klein, 1984b[1940]) where the good and the bad of the organisation could be held internally. There was evidence, too, of a pathological response to organisational death akin to melancholy. In Chapter Five, I identified those within the organisation who adopted a melancholic stance and failed to work through their loss. Paranoid–schizoid thinking (Klein, 1984b[1940]) and basic assumption work behaviour (Bion, 1961) were evidenced in this melancholic response. Here, denial, greed, splitting, and mania were defences employed against the pain of organisational death.

My analysis in Chapter Six demonstrated that the death drive, in both its forms, has relevance for an organisation at its end, in the wish to return to nothingness and in the drive to destruction. Manic reparation (Klein, 1984b[1940]), aggression, and the expression of envy (Klein, 1957), as well as basic assumption behaviour fight/flight (Bion, 1961), manifested itself. I found organisation location impacts on the way in which loss was experienced. Within the City of London, the bank was one of many organisations that had failed and that were subject to collapse; this taint led to an expression of the death drive as a return to nothingness, a primal wish to escape and dissolve. The experience of ending in the organisation related to the experience of the broader stage of the City of London. In the international headquarters, the death drive was expressed more violently. Here, the collapse brought the aggressive and sadistic elements of the death drive to the fore. Chapter Seven examined the defences against death employed to protect employees and to soothe the anxiety of the end.

Application of Freud to organisational death

Freud's death work can be utilised in examining organisational death. Adopting a position of denial, defences against death, projection, and working through the relevance of Freudian death work to organisational endings has been demonstrated.

Denial of death

Organisations believe in their immortality and, like humans, find it difficult to engage with the prospect of their own death, Freud would describe this as *an impossibility*. The notion of the impossibility of death, even when facing death, as captured in Damien Hirst's shark preserved in formaldehyde, can be translated to a denial of organisational death. Organisations persist with narcissistic notions of organisational survival. My analysis has shown that Interbank saw itself in this immortal fashion: witnessing other organisations failing, it persisted in the behaviour and idea that it *cannot happen to us, we will survive, our share price will pick up, we will get over this*. This denial could be seen as a manic defence, a delusion of strength and superiority. This links to the compulsion to repeat in the boom and bust culture of the City, where memories are short and confidence is quickly restored. The denial of death could, in itself, be seen as a defence but is presented here as a failure to acknowledge the very idea of organisational death.

Defences

The research found that even when the end was nigh, individuals within the organisation resisted death; they adopted defences against death. These were found to manifest themselves in a number of ways. The importance of fun at work led to a manic jollity, a need to be amused and distracted as a way of coping with the stress of the end. The head of the department was regularly seen prowling the team looking, and asking, for tasty morsels of humour to distract and reassure. Humour was employed to create an atmosphere of fun; planning for the future ignores the absence of a future. Mania was also evidenced in the scheduling of meetings, creating of procedures, and commitment to order, monitoring internet use, sickness leave, planning, recruiting, and promoting. Food featured strongly, a feeding frenzy that never satisfies but offered some comfort and protection to the individuals from the reality of the end. My analysis has shown that within Interbank this range of defences was adopted, allowing individuals to continue to function and providing a buffer between their experience of work and the prospect of the end.

Projection

When moving closer to the acknowledgement of the impending end, there was anger. Questions were asked as to who was to blame for the closure of the organisation. Splitting was employed to differentiate from those good, honest, and hardworking employees who had no part to play in the closure and the dishonest, greedy, and ineffective executives responsible for the end of the workplace. Employees were found to have benefited greatly from the corruption of the banking system and yet, when things turned sour, there was a distance placed between their role in the bank and the actions of the leaders, the City, and the world economy. This projection represents an unstable and immature solution to unrecognised unconscious conflict—an exaggeration intended to soothe. Blame is apportioned and scapegoating takes place. Greed is derided and projected outside of the self. The research has illustrated the different ways in which people within organisations condemned to death respond and that one response is to direct anger and aggression outside, to separate themselves and the organisation from failure and greed.

Working through

For those able to work through the loss, there is a process of mourning and acceptance. The loss can be painful and difficult to navigate, but it can be acknowledged and internalised. There is a means to move beyond the death of the organisation. With this response to loss there might be anger, but the anger is not destructive and is expressed and processed—there is acceptance. In mourning, the self exists beyond the loss of the object, in this case, in the possibility of a working life outside Interbank. In melancholia, however, there is an inability to move forward and the process of working through is left hanging. The work has shown the different ways in which death is dealt with in an organisation facing closure. On the one hand, there are those who can accept the end and work with the consequences of closure, including contemplating a new working life outside of Interbank. On the other hand, for those who remain stuck in the melancholic state, unable to externalise the loss, the death of the organisation remains part of that employee and moving forward is unfathomable.

The death drive

The death drive in a dying organisation is present in both its manifestations. The wish to ignore the horror of financial ruin, of job loss, of shame, and lost opportunity is presented in a return to a state of nothing, where no responsibilities or expectation are demanded. In the world of work in the City, in a return to indecision and an infant-like state, there are breakdowns and suicide. On the other side of the death drive is the aggression and violence of scorn, vengeance, and destruction. Much of Freudian understanding is linked to the erotic and the libidinal, but I have argued that the most fundamental of our instincts is a desire to return to a neutral, inorganic state, a condition in which we experience no anxiety, tension, or stress. Such longing surely has great relevance in organisation dynamics. This desire for self-annihilation has significance in organisational terms—the experience of wishing a function or a role one is attached to "to go away", "to dissolve", is a common fantasy. Annihilation can also be understood in the writing out of culpability in organisational problems, placing responsibility elsewhere and literally removing oneself from the drama.

Application of Freud's death work
to organisations: observing and applying

Distance is a useful tool in contemplating death. Close attachment and involvement in death can make thinking very difficult. This applies equally to organisational death, endings, and closure. When an organisation in which you work faces its end, loss is deeply entangled in everyday existence. Therefore, the ending is inevitably emotional and complex. As an outsider observing such endings, one's stance is on the edge, being outside the organisation provides a privileged platform from which to observe without getting caught up in the organisational defences, or, if you are caught up, then to be able to reflect on this.

This distance equally applies to those working with an organisation facing closure and such insight can help those who are part of the organisational closure to move forward and work through their loss.

The City

The City of London cast its eyes away from the crisis: the analysis of the boom, bust, and boom cycle of events in the financial heartland. The City does not necessarily learn from its past mistakes. This has been linked to the inability to contemplate organisational mortality despite the warning signs throughout the world. Queen Elizabeth II's remark in October 2008, "Why did no one see it coming?", captured this denial succinctly. There are other ways in which the City turned away, even turned inwards, in retreat.

In examining Thanatos, I have shown how the death drive can be expressed in two very different ways: first as a desire to return to nothingness, to an inorganic state, presented first in Freud's engagement with death in *Beyond the Pleasure Principle* (1920g) and, second, as a more violent drive to destruction, presented in Freud's later analysis of *Civilization and its Discontents* (1930a). The City displayed more of the former than the latter—this was conveyed in the analysis of Interbank and in the climate of the City beyond the crisis.

The City buried its head, returned to the womb, and rocked itself into a numbing state of denial. The suicides within Interbank and the City can be understood in the light of the wish to return to a state of nothingness (Cederstrom & Fleming, 2012, Cullen, 2014). As identified, for Freud, suicide represented the killing off of the unwanted self (1912–1913). There were other signs that the City expressed the characteristics of the death drive associated with a return to nothingness rather than the more aggressive, sadistic elements of the death drive evidenced in the headquarters of the bank. The City of London based bank immersed itself in numbing procedures and bureaucracy. Planning, meetings, and attention to process and quality control allowed this organisation to bury its head and itself firmly in the ground.

Interbank–New Interbank

Within Interbank, the ending was experienced differently by employees and teams; the split was akin to the response of mourning or melancholia. The employees who were recruited with the expectation of a lifetime career are contrasted with the shorter-term employees who joined the organisation in the knowledge that the bank was in a slow closure process. Unlike longer-term employees, these recruits were fully aware that their time in the organisation was limited from the outset and that their employment was unlikely to result in a long-term future. These groups offered a helpful distinction in dealing with the loss of the organisation. There was also a polarised response to the crushing reality. Leaders were blamed or idealised, organisational tactics justified as not understood by those outside. The insiders and outsiders, liars and truth tellers, innovators and bureaucrats, were divided and blamed.

An organisation is made up of many individuals who experience their loss in different ways, so an operating system could contain individuals who are mournful and others who are melancholic. This is a mirror representation of family life, where members of the same family experience their loss differently based on a number of factors, including psychical makeup, valance, relationship to the deceased, etc. In Interbank, this was the case, although the greater volume of data spoke to a melancholic response. I have shown how the members of the organisation were split in their response to their ending. In melancholia, there is an inability to replace the lost object with any new object of love; if we apply this to organisational death, the object becomes the impossibility of the prospect or actuality of another place of work. It further shows links between the melancholic self-reproach and the sense of responsibility and blame directed at the self for the organisation's downfall. Thus, the thesis illustrates the way in which "what starts outside comes in" (Frosh, 2012, p. 132) and how "the shadow of the object fell upon the ego" (Freud, 1917e, p. 249).

The way in which people mourn the loss of organisational life was contrasted with a melancholic response where the defences against death are evidenced and presented in emergent themes of mania, denial, greed, and splitting. Each of these themes was examined and examples narrated. Their contribution to understanding organisational death was explained. What emerges is an organisation of greed and gorging contrasted with an organisation of delusion and denial; an organisation that was loyal to a charismatic leader, yet also accepting of the end, an organisation working through.

Reflections on my role as researcher

Psychodynamic exploration sits in an interpretative paradigm and there is an impossibility of objectivity; the aim of the quality of the research is expressed in terms of plausibility (Frosh & Emerson, 2005). The role of the researcher in the data gathering process is integral to the outcome of the research project and, as such, this requires attention in the first person—this was an intensely personal piece of work. Building on Armstrong's (2005) explanation of a psychoanalytic approach to working with organisations as a consultant, I suggest that the researcher aims to disclose the inner world of the organisation through the inner world of the researcher.

Recognising, with searing pain, the reality of who we are is at the heart of psychoanalysis. The defences we adopt are there to protect ourselves from that painful reality. During the research, my focus was on the individuals within the organisation. I now turn that attention inward and reflect on my own part in the research process. Stapley (1996) encourages the consultant to adopt curiosity and self-knowledge, to be able to rely on an understanding of one's own unconscious, what belongs to the consultant and what belongs to the client. In researching using a psychoanalytic approach, self-knowledge and understanding of unconscious processes at play is equally important.

The ideal analyst and researcher are similarly employed making use of the observed behaviour, the disturbances produced by the observation itself, and their emotional reactions and behaviour of the observer (Devereux, 1967). This was the basis of this research project. Like the analyst, the analytically orientated researcher must be able to occupy a position where the capacity to think is maintained, recognising and tolerating painful emotions that might be experienced in close quarters.

"Chronic niceness" is a term I referred to in connection with the work of staff at hospices, who are dealing with the issue of death on a daily basis. Such niceness with the patients leaves a gap for the negative aspects of the cruelty and unsavoury elements of death. In my role as researcher, I worked hard to be the "perfect researcher". I expressed appreciation, tried not to get in the way, and always stuck to the terms of my agreed presence in the organisation. I explore here the different roles I held for the organisation and the function of the researcher as parasite, where "In the parasitic association even friendliness is deadly" (Bion, 1985, p. 131).

Representations of the researcher to the organisation

What I represented to the organisation is worthy of reflection. In allowing an outsider in at a delicate time, there might have been a message of "we have nothing to hide". The sense of shame expressed by some during the research might well have been masked by this generous hospitality. An organisation that has no future is still orientated to the future by allowing an academic researcher space within its walls. I recognise that I held different roles during the observation: as witness, ally, container for hostility, decoration, and a symbol of the world outside, an afterlife.

As an outsider brought in by the head of department, I held some value for Anna. She displayed great willingness to assist in the research, making introductions to individuals whom she thought I would find interesting to interview, opening up her team for me to observe, and allowing me to sit in on regular team meetings. On the surface, this could be interpreted as an altruistic act, one that was carried out for the greater good, for education, and out of kindness to an associate. These motivations might well have been present, but the likelihood is that I also held something else for Anna. One possibility is that I was an escape valve to the outside world—a symbol of life outside the organisation.

I might have been seen as an emblem of another life, and one that was focused on a future contribution (i.e., I was working as a researcher with the aim of adding to knowledge and new thought). Perhaps, also, I might have been seen as holding some kind of understanding or solution to the difficulties she was encountering in the workplace. I can also hypothesise that I had value as a witness to the challenges and trauma she experienced and that I could be held as an ally in vulnerable times. Anna constantly introduced me as her friend.

This elicited different responses in me. On many occasions, I felt a wish to create a distance and maintain my professionalism. On others, I was charmed and flattered by her attention. However, I was aware of being used for this purpose and the unspoken agreement between us that reflected our mutual benefit to each other.

Bick (1964) writes that the new mother frequently comments on the value of having regular visitors to her home with whom she could speak about her baby and her feelings towards the infant. As a regular visitor to the organisation, the role I held for the team was, I believe, more complex. For some, I was an object of hostility. Perhaps the extended length of the observation meant that the initial welcome and warmth literally expired. There might well also have been an expectation for insights and support that were not forthcoming. Reminiscent of an experiential group that turns with need to the consultant to lead and guide the group (Bion, 1961), this group was disappointed. Its hostility was, in this way, born out of disappointment in my failure to rescue the group.

I also noted by the lifts and at the points of entry and departure that there was interest in my appearance. My clothes, accessories, etc., were commented on—often by Anna, but also by the rest of the department. Perhaps, in this way, I served as some kind of decoration, an ornament to distract and elicit admiring or evaluative glances every so often. I could also have been seen as a balm, the researcher giving the organisation the attention it lacked. It was sick and I tended to its frailty (Leader & Corfield, 2008).

From the start of the research until the end, I felt a strong sense of privilege; my vantage point as observer in an organisation in the midst of such unusual crises, located at the heart of the broader national and international crisis, did indeed feel fortunate. The ease with which I was able to access interviewees and adopt my observation position over a long period was an aspect of the study that I did not take for granted. While I adopted a position of privilege, it was one I undertook with a real sense of responsibility. I was aware of the power of my position in other ways, too. Those I was observing were working in an environment that would cease to exist in the near future. My work was based on capitalising on their experience of that loss to create greater personal and academic opportunities. This did lead to some feelings of guilt and discomfort.

Researcher as parasite

In the eyes of the organisation, I had become integrated with the organisation as a whole, I was seen as a regular feature, a passive but constant being. My acceptance into the structure of the workplace is reflected in the following observation note.

> The receptionist tells him that she is sure I have my own badge. I say no, I am issued with a badge every time I come in, and she says again no, I have seen a badge with her picture on.

The receptionist, who sees me week after week, is so sure that I am part of the organisation that she imagines she has actually seen a security pass with my photograph on it. It seems that I had seeped into her unconscious as a part of the corporate structure. During my stay, I happily fed off the multiple offerings, the blood, heart, and soul of the organisation.

> In the parasitic relationship, the product of the association is something that destroys both parties to the association. The realization that approximates most closely to my formulation is the group–individual setting dominated by envy. Envy begets envy and this self-perpetuating emotion finally destroys host and parasite alike. The envy cannot be satisfactorily ascribed to one or other party; in fact, it is a function of the relationship. (Bion, 1985, p. 131)

The parasitic relationship kills of both parties eventually. The host is damaged by the parasite and the parasite cannot survive without the host. In the context of the research, the organisation "killed me off" shortly before it ceased to exist itself. Effectively, I feasted on the flesh of their death and benefited enormously from the process. While I attempted to do this in as reasonable a manner as possible, it remains the case that I continued to live on in my role and they did not. Inevitably, that reality would stir up some feelings of resentment and anger, perhaps compounded by my image of niceness and professionalism.

Bion provides the powerful analogy of the animating maggot: "I think there is always a resistance to development and change and a tendency to think what a horrible thing this maggot is that tries to animate the dung heap" (Bion, 1976, p. 278).

The parasite can serve a useful function in breaking down matter; I had failed to offer anything to the host. I had exploited the hospitality of the organisation, yet failed to deliver the comfort of a consultant or visitor who might have helped to cope with the difficulties by aiding understanding or offering insights into the activities I observed. Interpretation can be offered to analytic patients as a means to modify anxiety (Klein, 1932), but this balm was not available to the people I observed and interviewed and there is some angst in taking from the process that typically involves an expressed interpretation to process matters. I was a guest who had made themselves at home, yet failed to conform to conventional behaviour and offer something tangible in return for their hospitality. In analysis, the process of transference and countertransference is conducted to allow the analysand to better know and understand themselves. Or, as Bion expressed it, "To introduce the patient to the most important person he is ever likely to have dealings with, namely himself" (1978, p. 5). This gift of self-knowledge was not shared with the participants in my research and is a regret. The ethics procedures were followed meticulously, yet would participants have been resistant had they known more about the way in which the data would be treated? I am aware that such a gift might well have been unwanted.

In summary

The City of London has seen boom and bust and is currently emerging from the financial crisis. The impact of Brexit and global political uncertainty are not yet known. What is likely is that further organisational collapse will be endured, whatever political and economic decisions are made.

Death in the City has presented death as both an essential life event that must be considered and confronted and as something that is impossible to hold in our unconscious. "*Si vis vitam, para mortem*: if you want to endure life, prepare yourself for death" (Freud, 1915b, pp. 299–300). This urges humankind to live their life, but to do so in the shadow of death. So, in the City of London, the collapse of a financial institution has demonstrated ways of living: with aggression and violence and with denial and retreat under the shadow of organisational death.

The compulsion to repeat shows us that destructive patterns of behaviour are repeated again and again and the way in which this is reflected in the boom and bust of the City of London has been illustrated. We must question, was this collapse truly unanticipated or were the good times just too good to let go? Were workers in the City lacking an ability to adopt a third position, to imagine a possibility that the good times were not going to last forever and that disaster was possible; had they lost the capacity "for reflecting on ourselves whilst being ourselves (Britton, 1989, p. 87)? The unconscious behaviour of the group of workers in the City, colluding with the deception of a continual rise in fortune, can also be viewed as a large work group operating in Bion's basic assumption dependency mode (1961), the icon of the City as the embodiment of a leading symbol that could not fail to lead them to nirvana.

The social and economic setting of this research is important. The work began in the aftermath of the financial crisis when the City of London had experienced protests (for example, the G20 summit protest, April 2009, and the Occupy London movement during the closing months of 2011 and into 2012). Bankers have been portrayed as the new dirty workers (Stanley, 2012) and were seen as greedy, fat cats, gamblers, and criminals. The greed associated with bankers in particular was a key feature of the dissection of bankers' pay and bonuses, eliciting strong and violent reactions. Those who participated in the research interviews were aware of this labelling and were keen to distinguish themselves from the high earning few, or those who worked at investment banks, particularly on trading desks. There was a wish to portray themselves as ordinary, hard-working professionals. It was hard for them to see the greed that existed in themselves and far easier to project that into a privileged few.

The disappointment of the city

The following vignette from the observation, noted in June 2012, captures the essence of moving on and disappointment with the City of London.

> A parcel arrives—a long white cardboard tube. This, Anna explains to no one in particular, is a leaving gift for someone on another floor who is very nosy and would have found out what it was. She calls Ben on the telephone and explains that the parcel has arrived. He comes up to the floor, opens the package, and unrolls a poster of London detailed in black ink. He says the quality is not what he expected; he thought it would be a bit sharper. Anna and Ben pore over the map, he expressing his disappointment, she agreeing.

The choice of gift, an ink drawing of the City of London, destined for an executive who is leaving his post because of the collapse of the bank, is a disappointment. But the disappointment does not seem to speak only to the quality of the poster, but also to the City of London.

This is not what was expected, the quality should have been better, the finish sharper, the detail considered. The City has disappointed.

> "It was very prestigious. Completely the opposite of what came down the road to what it is now. So as I said, it was a bit of a utopia. You should have thought how could it last? It didn't last."

This research has shown that an organisation, and the people in it, can be both mournful and melancholic. There is a distinction between mourning and melancholia: mourning is the painful but inevitable grief that comes with the loss of a loved person (object) associated with mourning, a process that concludes with a commitment to live on, in effect to triumph in some way over the loss. Melancholia differs in that the sufferer's inability to separate from the lost person (or object) results in their remaining trapped. Ambivalence in mourning and melancholia is presented as a struggle between the wish to be with the living and the wish to be at one with the dead. Together with the former is the pain of grief and loss and the knowledge that the mourner's own capacity for life is at stake. The mourner is able to "kill off" the object, therefore freeing the individual to grieve and mourn for that lost object. The melancholic holds on to the object, in effect "deadening" him or herself by wishing to be with that object.

Within the organisation, the employees could be split into those who adopted a melancholic stance, and those with a mournful response to the loss of both the ideal of the organisation and their actual career. Their ambivalence left them straddling the path between life and death, clinging to their identities and careers, yet nursing huge losses and the need to gain new employment.

The global financial crisis of 2008 and beyond challenged the deeply rooted notion of the economy as a highly rational and predictable market. Despite the presumed rationality of economic theory, most recognise a psychological, even psychical, dimension to the events leading up to the crash. Denial, self-interest, narcissism, envy, greed, power, and fantasy might all be employed to interpret events of the crash.

Psychoanalytic theory derives from Freud's realisation that attempts to understand neurosis by focusing on a study of fundamental discovery was that the shift of focus to the analyst–patient dyad and to the transaction between the two—the transference and the countertransference—could uncover rich material that was held in the patient's unconscious. The dyadic relation was an "intelligible field of study" (Bion, 1961, p. 104). As a result, Freud and his successors have given us a much deeper understanding of the processes of human development from infancy onwards and of the ways in which they shape our perceptions and relationships as adults.

Death and loss are not restricted to personal and familial mortality. The mortal subject examined here presents death of an object of attachment of any kind: loss of identity, employment, and purpose through the death of the organisation to which one once belonged. The concept of mourning applied to those experiencing the loss of work and organisation has been brought forward. This writing has pursued the argument for the relevance of loss, mourning, melancholia, and death at work.

As the objects of my observation endured the slow closure of their organisation and lived week by week, month by month with the knowledge of impending organisational death, so, too, have I been intensely involved with the death of the organisation and of my research. Being immersed in death could be interpreted as deflating and miserable; however, I join with Freud: by engaging in the reality of death, life has a different quality, and life is shallower and diminished without the acknowledgement of death.

Freud speaks of the possibility that greater truthfulness and honesty could pave the way to transforming relations between people (1916a). Yet, this hopeful conclusion does not match the illogical blindness often forced on employees by their reaction to the crises unfolding before their eyes and their defences against death and resistance to the inevitable closure of their hopes and aspirations. Death is not at a distance, and large and small losses are constantly with us. In a working climate where endings, loss, and organisational closure will feature prominently, tackling death at work has relevance and potency. By engaging with the prospect of death, greater thought can be given to connecting with loss and the consequences of that loss. Paradoxically, that engagement can create greater opportunity for life, for aliveness.

REFERENCES

Akhtar, S. (2011). *Matters of Life and Death: Psychoanalytic Reflections*. London: Karnac.

Allen, M. T. (2002). *The Business of Genocide: The SS, Slave Labor, and the Concentration Camps*. Chapel Hill, NC: University of North Carolina Press.

Allen, M. T. (2005). Grey-collar worker: organisation theory in Holocaust studies. *Holocaust Studies: A Journal of Culture and History*, 11(1): 27–53.

Allen, M. T. (2008). The atomization of Auschwitz: is history really that contingent? http://michaelthadallen.comHomepage.pages/articles/L&L.

Altman, Y., & Baruch, Y. (2010). The organizational lunch. *Culture and Organization*, 16(2): 127–143.

Archer, J. (1999). *The Nature of Grief. The Evolution and Psychology of Reactions to Loss*. London: Routledge.

Arendt, H. (1963). *Eichmann in Jerusalem: A Report on the Banality of Evil*. London: Faber and Faber.

Arman, R. (2014). Death metaphors and factory closure. *Culture and Organization*, 20(1): 23–39.

Armstrong, D. (2005). *Organisation in the Mind*. London: Karnac.

Bakan, J. (2005). *The Corporation: The Pathological Pursuit of Profit and Power*. London: Simon and Schuster.

Banerjee, S. B. (2008). Necrocapitalism. *Organizational Studies, 29*(12): 1541–1563.

Barbash, T. (2006). A tale of renewal: for the 9/11 survivors of Cantor Fitzgerald, working to rebuild their firm has been the key to healing. *Business Week,* September 11: 84–86.

Bauer, Y. (2001). *Rethinking the Holocaust.* New Haven, CT: Yale University Press.

Bauman, Z. (1989). *Modernity and the Holocaust.* Ithaca, NY: Cornell University.

Bell, E., & Taylor, S. (2011). Beyond letting go and moving on: new perspectives on organizational death, loss and grief, *Scandinavian Journal of Management, 27*: 1–10.

Bell, E., & Taylor, S. (2012). Emotionalized interactions with technology: mourning for Steve Jobs. Paper presented to the Academy of Management Conference, Boston, August.

Benjamin, J. (1988). *The Bonds of Love: Psychoanalysis, Feminism, and the Problem of Domination.* New York: Pantheon.

Bennett, D. (2012). *Loaded Subjects. Psychoanalysis, Money and the Global Financial Crisis.* London: Lawrence & Wishart.

Bergman, P., & Wigblad, R. (1999). Workers last performance: why some factories show their best results during countdown. *Journal of Economic and Industrial Democracy, 20*(3): 343–368.

Bick, E. (1964). Notes on infant observation in psychoanalytic training. *International Journal of Psychoanalysis, 45*: 558–566.

Bion, W. R. (1961). *Experiences in Groups.* London: Tavistock.

Bion, W. R. (1976). In interview with A. G. Banet. *Group & Organization Studies, 9*(3): 268–285.

Bion, W. R. (1978). *Four Discussions with W. R. Bion.* StrathTay: Blairgowrie.

Bion, W. R. (1985). Container and contained. *Group Relations Reader, 2*: 127–133.

Blau, G. (2006). A process model for understanding victim responses to worksite/function closure. *Human Resource Management Review, 16*(1): 12–28.

Blau, G. (2007). Partially testing a process model for understanding victim responses to an anticipated worksite closure. *Journal of Vocational Behaviour, 7*(3): 401–428.

Blau, G. (2008). Exploring antecedents of individual grieving stages during an anticipated worksite closure. *Journal of Occupational and Organizational Psychology, 81*: 529–550.

Blok, A. (2001). *Honour and Violence.* Cambridge: Polity Press.

Bollas, C. (1987). *The Shadow of the Object: Psychoanalysis of the Unthought Known*. London: Free Association Books.

Bowlby, J. (1960). Grief and mourning in infancy and early childhood. *Psychoanalytic Study of the Child, 15*: 9–52.

Bowlby, J. (1961). The process of mourning. *International Journal of Psychoanalysis, 42*: 317–340.

Bowlby, J. (1980). *Loss: Sadness and Depression*. New York: Basic Books.

Bowlby, J., & Parkes, C. M. (1970). Separation and loss within the family. The child in his family. In: *International Yearbook of Child Psychiatry and Allied Professions* (pp. 197–216). New York: Wiley.

Britton, R. (1989). The missing link: parental sexuality in the Oedipus complex. In: *The Oedipus Complex Today: Clinical Implications* (pp. 83–101). London: Karnac.

Canham, H. (2002). Group and gang states of mind. *Journal of Child Psychotherapy, 28*: 113–127.

Carr, A., & Lapp, C. (2006). *Leadership Is a Matter of Life and Death. The Psychodynamics of Eros and Thanatos Working in Organizations*. New York: Palgrave Macmillan.

Carroll, G., & Delacroix, J. (1982). Organizational mortality in the newspaper industries in Argentina and Ireland: an ecological approach. *Administrative Science Quarterly, 27*: 169–198.

Cederstrom, C., & Fleming, P. (2012). *Dead Man Working*. Winchester: Zero Books.

Clegg, S., Kornberger, M., & Rhodes, C. (2007). Business ethics as practice. *British Journal of Management, 18*: 107–122.

Cohen, J. (2005). *How to Read Freud*. London: Granta Books.

Coltart, N. (1989). Personal communication. In: J. Berke (Ed.), *The Tyranny of Malice: Exploring the Dark Side of Character* (pp. 26–27). London: Simon & Schuster.

Comfort, N. (2013). *The Slow Death of British Industry*. London: Biteback.

Cullen, J. (2014). Towards an organisational suicidology, *Culture & Organization, 20*(1): 40–52.

Cunningham, J. B. (1997). Feelings and interpretations during an organization's death. *Journal of Organizational Change Management, 10*(6): 471–490.

Daft, R. L. (2004). *Organization Theory and Design*. Manson, Ohio: Thomson South-Western.

Devereux, G. (1967). *From Anxiety to Method in Behavioural Sciences*. New York: Humanities Press.

Dollimore, J. (2001). *Death, Desire and Loss in Western Culture*. New York: Routledge.

Douglas, D. (2004). The lived experience of loss: a phenomenological study. *Journal of the American Psychiatric Nurses Association, 10*: 24–32.

Driver, M. (2007). Meaning and suffering in organizations. *Journal of Organizational Change Management, 20*(5): 611–632.

Driver, M. (2008). Every bite you take . . . food and the struggles of embodied subjectivity in organizations. *Human Relations, 61*: 913–934.

Driver, M. (2009). From loss to lack: stories of organizational change as encounters with failed fantasies of self, work and organization. *Organization, 16*: 487–504.

Eigen, M. (1995). The destructive force within. *Contemporary Psychoanalysis, 31*: 603–616.

Eigen, M. (2004)[1966]. *Psychic Deadness*. London: Karnac.

Eissler, K. R. (1978). Creativity and adolescence: the effect of trauma in Freud's adolescence. *Psychoanalytic Study of the Child*, 0079–7308, psycnet.apa.org

Elrod, D. P., & Tippett, D. D. (2002). The death valley of change. *Journal of Organizational Change Management, 15*(3): 273–291.

Feldman, M. (2000). Some views on the manifestation of the death instinct in clinical work. *International Journal of Psychoanalysis, 81*: 53–65.

Fotaki, M., Long, S., & Schwartz, H. (2012). What can psychoanalysis offer organization studies today? Taking stock of current developments and thinking about future directions. *Organization Studies, 33*(9), Special Issue: 1105–1120.

Freud, S. (1900a). *The Interpretation of Dreams. S. E.*, 4–5. London: Hogarth Press.

Freud, S. (1905d). *Three Essays on the Theory of Sexuality. S. E., 5*: 125–245. London: Hogarth Press.

Freud, S. (1912–1913). *Totem and Taboo. S. E., 13*. London: Hogarth Press.

Freud, S. (1914g). Remembering, repeating and working-through. *S. E., 12*: 145–156. London: Hogarth.

Freud, S. (1915b). Thoughts for the times on war and death. *S. E., 14*: 275–300. London: Hogarth Press.

Freud, S. (1915c). Instincts and their vicissitudes. *S. E., 14*: 109–140. London: Hogarth Press.

Freud, S. (1916a). On transience. *S. E., 14*: 303–307. London: Hogarth Press.

Freud, S. (1917e). Mourning and melancholia. *S. E., 14*: 239–258. London: Hogarth Press.

Freud, S. (1920g). *Beyond the Pleasure Principle. S. E., 18*: 7–64. London: Hogarth Press.

Freud, S. (1921c). *Group Psychology and the Analysis of the Ego. S. E., 18*: 65–144. London: Hogarth.

Freud, S. (1923b). *The Ego and the Id. S. E., 19*: 3–66. London: Hogarth Press.

Freud, S. (1926d). *Inhibitions, Symptoms and Anxiety. S. E., 20*: 77–174. London: Hogarth Press.

Freud, S. (1930a). *Civilization and its Discontents. S. E., 21*: 59–145. London: Hogarth Press.

Freud, S. (1933a/1974). *New Introductory Lectures on Psycho-analysis. S. E., 22*: 3–182. London: Hogarth Press.

Freud, S. (1933b). Why war? *S. E., 22*: 197–215. London: Hogarth Press.

Freud, S. (1937c). Analysis terminable and interminable. *S. E., 23*: 211–253. London: Hogarth Press.

Freud, S. (1940e). Splitting of the ego in the process of defence. *S. E., 23*: 273–285. London: Hogarth Press.

Freud, S. (1985). *The Complete Letters of Sigmund Freud to Wilhelm Fliess*, J. M. Mason (Ed. and Trans.). Cambridge, MA: Harvard University Press.

Frosh, S. (2012). *A Brief Introduction to Psychoanalytic Theory*. Basingstoke: Palgrave Macmillan.

Frosh, S., & Emerson, P. D. (2005). Interpretation and over-interpretation: disputing the meaning of texts. *Qualitative Research, 5*(3): 307–324.

Gabriel, Y. (1999). *Organizations in Depth*. London: Sage.

Gabriel, Y. (2012). Organizations in a state of darkness: towards a theory of organizational miasma. *Organization Studies, 33*(9): 1137–1152.

Galbraith, J. (1982). The stages of growth. *Journal of Business Strategy, 3*: 70–79.

Gould, L. J., Stapley, L. F., & Stein, M. (Eds.) (2001). *The Systems Psycho-dynamics of Organizations: Integrating the Group Relations Approach, Psychoanalytic and Open Systems Perspective*. London: Karnac.

Gould, P. (2011). *When I Die: Lessons from the Death Zone*. London: Little Brown.

Hansson, M. (2004). When the lights go out. Paper presented to the European Academy of Management Conference, May.

Hansson, M. (2008). On closedowns: towards a pattern of explanations to the closedown effect. PhD Dissertation, Swedish Business School, Orebro University.

Hansson, M., & Wigblad, R. (2006). Pyrrhic victories: anticipating the closedown effect. *International Journal of Human Resource Management, 17*(5): 938–959.

Hardy, C. (1985). *Managing Organizational Closure*. Farnham: Gower.

Harris, S. G., & Sutton, R. L. (1986). Functions of parting ceremonies in dying organizations. *Academy of Management Journal, 29*(1): 5–30.

Hasanen, L. (2010). Organizational death and employee motivation: investigating a plant closure in a multi-plant organization. Doctoral thesis, Stockholm University.

Hazen, M. A. (2008). Grief and the workplace. *Academy of Management Perspectives, August*: 78–86.

Hinshelwood, R. D. (1991). *A Dictionary of Kleinian Thought*. London: Free Association Books.

Hinshelwood, R. D., & Skogstad, W. (2000). *The Dynamics of Health Care Institutions. Observing Organisations: Anxiety, Defence and Culture in Health Care*. London: Routledge.

Hirschhorn, L. (1988). *The Workplace Within: Psychodynamics of Organizational Life*. Cambridge, MA: MIT Press.

Hirschhorn, L., & Gilmore, T. (1989). The psychodynamics of a cultural change. Learning from a factory. *Human Resource Management, 28*: 211–233.

Hirschman, A. O. (1970). *Exit, Voice, and Loyalty: Responses to Decline in Firms, Organizations, and States*. Cambridge, MA: Harvard University Press.

Hirst, D. (1991). *The Physical Impossibility of Death in the Mind of Someone Living*. Artwork commissioned in 1991 by Charles Saatchi, Glass, painted steel, silicone, monofilament, shark and formaldehyde solution.

Hollway, W., & Jefferson, T. (2000). *Doing Qualitative Research Differently: Free Association, Narrative and the Interview Method*. London: Sage.

Hollway, W., & Jefferson, T. (2012). *Doing Qualitative Research Differently: A Psychosocial Approach* (2nd edn). London: Sage.

Hyde, P., & Thomas, A. B. (2003). When a leader dies. *Human Relations, 56*(8): 1005–1024.

Jaques, E. (1988). Death and the mid-life crisis. In: E. B. Spillius (Ed.), *Melanie Klein Today: Developments in Theory and Practice, Volume 2: Mainly Practice* (pp. 226–248). London: Routledge.

Jervis, S. (2009). The use of self as a research tool. In: S. Clarke & P. Hoggett (Eds.), *Researching Beneath the Surface: Psycho-Social Research Methods in Practice* (pp. 145–166). London: Karnac.

Jones, E. (1961). *The Life and Work of Sigmund Freud*. Oxford: Basic Books.

Juda, D. P. (1983). Exorcising Freud's "daemonic" compulsion to repeat: repetition compulsion as part of the adaptational/maturational process. *Journal of the American Academy of Psychoanalysis, 11*(3): 353–375.

Kahn, S., & Liefooghe, A. (2014). Thanatos: Freudian manifestations of death at work. *Culture and Organization, 20*(1): 53–67.

Kelly, S., & Riach, K. (2012). Reanimating the dying organization: a study of materiality, bodies and myth in the UK financial services sector.

Presented to the Culture, Organizations and Markets Group Conference, 'Organizational death, memory and loss'. Keele University, 4–5 October.

Kets de Vries, M. F. R. (1989). *Prisoners of Leadership*. New York: Wiley.

Kets de Vries, M. F. R., & Balazs, K. (1997). The downside of downsizing. *Human Relations, 50*(1): 11–50.

Khanna, R. (2004). *Dark Continents: Psychoanalysis and Colonialism*, Durham, NC: Duke University Press.

Kindleberger, C. P., & Aliber, R. Z. (2011). *Manias, Panics and Crashes: A History of Financial Crises*. Basingstoke: Palgrave Macmillan.

Klein, M. (1932). *The Psychoanalysis of Children*. London: Hogarth.

Klein, M. (1946). Notes on some schizoid mechanisms. *International Journal of Psychoanalysis, 27*: 99–110.

Klein, M. (1948). A contribution to the theory of anxiety and guilt. *International Journal of Psychoanalysis, 29*: 112–123.

Klein, M. (1952). The origins of transference. In: *Envy and Gratitude and Other Works 1946–1963* (pp. 48–56). London: Virago.

Klein, M. (1957). *Envy and Gratitude and Other Works*. New York: Delta.

Klein, M. (1959). Our adult world and its roots in infancy. *Human Relations, 12*(4): 291–303.

Klein, M. (1975). Notes on some schizoid mechanisms. In: *The Writings of Melanie Klein Vol. 3: Envy and Gratitude and Other Works, 1946–1963* (pp. 1–24). London: Hogarth.

Klein, M. (1984a)[1935]. A contribution to the psychogenesis of manic-depressive states. In: *Love, Guilt and Reparation and Other Works* (pp. 344–369). London: Tavistock.

Klein, M. (1984b)[1940]. Mourning and its relation to manic-depressive states. In: *Love, Guilt and Reparation and Other Works* (pp. 344–369). London: Tavistock.

Kristeva, J. (1982). *Powers of Horror: An Essay on Abjection*. New York: Columbia University Press.

Kristeva, J. (2012). A tragedy and a dream: disability revisited. The Michael Devlin Lecture. In: *The Wounded Body: Human Vulnerability and Disability in a Finite World*. Maynooth, Ireland: Saint Patrick's College.

Krugman, P. (2008). *The Return of Depression Economics and the Crisis of 2008*. London: Penguin.

Kubler-Ross, E. (1969). *On Death and Dying*. New York: Scribner.

Lacan, J. (1988). *The Seminar of Jacques Lacan: Book II: The Ego in Freud's Theory and in the Technique of Psychoanalysis*. Cambridge: Cambridge University Press Archive.

Lakotta, B., & Schels, W. (2004). *Noch mal leben dem Tod*. Anstalt: Deutsche.

Lanchaster, J. (2010). *Whoops! Why Everyone Owes Everyone and No One Can Pay*. London: Penguin.

Laplanche, J. (1970). *Life and Death in Psychoanalysis*, Baltimore, MD: Johns Hopkins University Press.

Lawrence, W. G. (2000). Thinking refracted. In: *Tongued with Fire. Groups in Experience* (pp. 1–30). London: Karnac.

Lawson, D. (2009). The ultimate financial resource. www.independent.co.uk, 7 April.

Leader, D., & Corfield, D. (2008). *Why Do People Get Ill? Exploring the Mind–Body Connection*. London: Penguin.

Leana, C., & Feldman, D. C. (1988). Individual responses to job loss: perceptions, reactions, and coping behaviors. *Journal of Management*, 14(3): 375–389.

Lear, J. (1998). *Open Minded: Working Out the Logic of the Soul*. Cambridge, MA: Harvard University Press.

Lear, J. (2000). *Happiness, Death, and the Remainder of Life: The Tanner Lectures on Human Values*. Cambridge, MA: Harvard University Press.

Levine, D. P. (2001). The fantasy of inevitability in organizations. *Human Relations*, 54(10): 1251–1265.

Levine, D. P. (2005). The corrupt organization. *Human Relations*, 58(6): 723–740.

Levinson, H., Price, C., Munden, K., Mandl, H., & Solley, C. (1962). *Men, Management, and Mental Health*. Cambridge, MA: Harvard University Press.

Lewin, K. (1952). *Group Decision and Social Change. Readings in Social Psychology*. New York: Henry Holt.

Long, S. (2008). *The Perverse Organization and Its Deadly Sins*. London: Karnac.

Long, S., & Sievers, B. (2012). *Towards a Socioanalysis of Money, Finance and Capitalism: Beneath the Surface of the Financial Industry*. London: Routledge.

Lyotard, J. F. (1993). The other's rights. In: *On Human Rights* (pp. 135–149). New York: Basic Books.

Marcuse, H. (1955). *Eros and Civilization*. Boston, MA: Beacon.

Mellahi, K., & Wilkinson, A. (2004). Organizational failure: a critique of recent research and a proposed integrative framework. *International Journal of Management Reviews*, 5–6(1): 21–41.

Menzies Lyth, I. (1960). Social systems as a defence against anxiety: an empirical study of the nursing service of a general hospital. *Human Relations*, 13: 95–121.

Meyer, M. W., & Zucker, L. G. (1989). *Permanently Failing Organizations*. London: Sage.

Milgram, S. (1974). *Obedience to Authority: An Experimental View*. New York: Harper & Row.

Mills, R., Scott, J., Alati, R., O'Callaghan, M., & Najman, J. M. (2013). Child maltreatment and adolescent mental health problems in large birth cohorts. *Child Abuse and Neglect, 37*(5): 292–302.

Minsky, R. (1996). *Psychoanalysis and Gender: An Introductory Reader*. London: Routledge.

Moore, B. E., & Fine, B. D. (Eds.) (1990). *Psychoanalytic Terms and Concepts*. New Haven, CT: Yale University Press.

Moylan, D. (1994). The dangers of contagion: protective identification processes in institutions. In: A. Obholzer & V. Z. Roberts (Eds.), *The Unconscious at Work* (pp. 51–59). London: Routledge.

Noer, D. M. (1993). *Healing the Wounds: Overcoming the Trauma of Layoffs and Revitalizing Downsized Organizations*. San Francisco, CA: Jossey-Bass.

Ogden, T. H. (2012). *Creative Readings—Essays on Seminal Analytic Works*. London: Routledge.

Orwell, G. (1936). *Keep the Aspidistra Flying*. London: Penguin.

Parkes, C. M. (1972). *Bereavement: Studies of Grief in Adult Life*. New York: International Universities Press.

Perman, R. (2013). *Hubris: How HBOS Wrecked the Best Bank in Britain*. Edinburgh: Birlinn.

Piven, J. (2004). *Death and Delusion: A Freudian Analysis of Mortal Terror*. Greenwich, CT: Information Age.

Prebble, L. (2009). *Enron* (Play). London: Bloomsbury.

Queen Elizabeth II (2008). www.telegraph.co.uk>News>UK News>The Royal Family 05/11/2008.

Razinsky, L. (2013). *Freud, Psychoanalysis and Death*. Cambridge: Cambridge University Press.

Rosenfeld, H. A. (1971). A clinical approach to the psychoanalytic theory of the life and death instincts: an investigation into the aggressive aspects of narcissism. In: J. Steiner (Ed.), *Rosenfeld in Retrospect: Essays On His Clinical Influence* (pp. 116–130). London & New York: Routledge.

Rycroft, C. (1962). Beyond the reality principle. *International Journal of Psychoanalysis, 43*: 388–394.

Rycroft, C. (1995). *Critical Dictionary of Psychoanalysis*. London: Penguin.

Salzberger-Wittenberg, I. (2013). *Experiencing Endings and Beginnings*. London: Karnac.

Samuel, Y. (2010). *Organizational Pathology, Life and Death of Organizations*. New Brunswick, Canada: Transaction.

Schopenhauer, A. (1966)[1819/1844]. *The World as Will and Representation*. New York: Dover.

Schwartz, H. S. (1992). *Narcissistic Process and Corporate Decay: The Theory of the Organization Ideal*. New York: New York University Press.

Scott, W. R. (1992). *Organizations: Rational, Natural and Open Systems* (3rd edn). Englewood Cliffs, NJ: Prentice-Hall.

Segal, H. (1958). Fear of death: notes on the analysis of an old man. *International Journal of Psychoanalysis, 39*: 178–181.

Seneca, (1997). *On the Shortness of Life*, C. D. N. Costa (Trans.). London: Penguin.

Seshadri-Crooks, K. (2000). *Desiring Whiteness: A Lacanian Analysis of Race*. London: Routledge.

Sheppard, J. P. (1994). Strategy and bankruptcy: an exploration into organizational death. *Journal of Management, 20*(4): 795–833.

Sher, M. (2013). *The Dynamics of Change: Tavistock Approaches to Improving Social Systems*. London: Karnac.

Sievers, B. (1994). *Work, Death and Life Itself: Essays on Management and Organization*. Berlin: Walter de Gruyter.

Sievers, B. (1999). Psychotic organization as a metaphoric frame for the socioanalysis of organizational and interorganizational dynamics. *Administration and Society, 31*(5): 588–615.

Sievers, B. (2003). Your money or your life? *Human Relations, 56*: 187

Sievers, B. (2012). Socio-analytic reflections on capitalist greed. *Organisational and Social Dynamics, 12*(1): 44–69, 129.

Simmel, E. (1944). Self-preservation and the death instinct. *Psychoanalytic Quarterly, 13*: 16–185.

Smith, L. (1994). Burned-out bosses. *Fortune, 130*(2): 100–105.

Sorkin, A. (2009). *Too Big to Fail: Inside the Battle to Save Wall Street*. London: Penguin.

Speck, P. (1994). Working with dying people. In: A. Obholzer & V. Z. Roberts (Eds.), *The Unconscious at Work* (pp. 94–100). London: Routledge.

Spielrein, S. (1994)[1912]. Destruction as the cause of coming into being. *Journal of Analytical Psychology, 39*(2): 155–186.

Spillius, E., Milton, J., Garvey, P., & Couve, C. (2011). *The New Dictionary of Kleinian Thought*. London: Routledge.

Stanley, E. (2012). "Scumbag millionaires": the rhetorical construction and resistance of stigma during the financial crisis. PhD Thesis, Birkbeck, University of London.

Stapley, L. F. (1996). *The Personality of the Organisation*. London: Free Association Books.

Stapley, L. F. (2006). *Individuals, Groups and Organizations Beneath the Surface: An Introduction*. London: Karnac.

Stapley, L. F., & Roberts, V. (2000). 'In end is my beginning': the changing context of psychoanalytically orientated consultancy. Presented to the 17th ISPSO Annual Symposium Presentation, London.

Stein, H. F. (1998). *Euphemism, Spin, and the Crisis in Organizational Life*. Westport, CT: Quorum.

Stein, H. F. (2001). *Nothing Personal, Just Business: A Guided Journey into Organizational Darkness*. Westport, CT: Quorum.

Stein, H. F. (2009). Death imagery and the experience of organizational downsizing or, is your name on Schindler's list? In: B. Sievers (Ed.), *Psychoanalytic Studies of Organizations* (pp. 123–151). London: Karnac.

Stein, M. (2000). After Eden: envy and the defences against anxiety paradigm. *Human Relations*, *53*(2): 193–211.

Stein, M. (2003). Unbounded irrationality: risk and organizational narcissism at long term capital management. *Human Relations*, *56*(5): 523–540.

Stein, M. (2007). Oedipus Rex at Enron: leadership, oedipal struggles, and organizational collapse. *Human Relations*, *60*: 1387–1410.

Stein, M. (2011). A culture of mania: a psychoanalytic view of the incubation of the 2008 credit crisis. *Organization*, *18*: 173–198.

Stein, M., & Pinto, J. (2011). The dark side of groups: a "gang at work" in Enron. *Group & Organization Management*, *36*: 692–721.

Steiner, J. (2008). The repetition compulsion, envy, and the death instinct. In: *Envy and Gratitude Revisited* (pp. 131–151). London: Karnac.

Stokes, J. (1994). The unconscious at work in groups and teams: contributions from the work of Wilfred Bion. In: A. Obholzer & V. Z. Roberts (Eds.), *The Unconscious at Work* (pp. 56–66). London: Routledge.

Stokes, P., & Gabriel, Y. (2010). Engaging with genocide: the challenge for organization and management studies. *Organization*, *17*: 461–480.

Stone, O. (Dir.) (1987). *Wall Street* (Film). 20th Century Fox.

Struckler, D., Basu, S., Suhrcke, M., Coutts, A., & McKee, M. (2011). Effects of the 2008 recession on health: a first look at European data. *The Lancet*, *378*(9786): 124–125.

Sutton, R. I. (1987). The process of organizational death—'disbanding and reconnecting'. *Administrative Science Quarterly*, *32*(4): 542–569.

Terry, A. W. (2012). My journey in grief: a mother's experience following the death of her daughter. *Qualitative Inquiry*, *18*: 355–367.

Tett, G. (2009). *Fool's Gold: How the Bold Dream of a Small Tribe at JP Morgan Was Corrupted by Wall Street Greed and Unleashed a Catastrophe*. London: Little, Brown.

Tuckett, D. (2007). Civilization and its discontents today. In: L. Braddock & M. Lacewing (Eds.), *The Academic Face of Psychoanalysis* (pp. 69–91). London: Routledge.

Turner, B. A. (1978). *Man-made Disasters*. London: Wykeham.

Turner, B. A., & Pidgeon, N. F. (1997). *Man-made Disasters*. Oxford: Butterworth-Heinemann.

Uchitelle, L. (2006). *The Disposable American: Layoffs and Their Consequences*. New York: Knopf.

Unruh, D. (1983). Death and personal history: strategies of self preservation. *Social Problems, 30*(3): 340–351.

Volkan, V. D. (2007). Not letting go: from individual perennial mourners to societies with entitlement ideologies In: L. Glocer Fiorini, S. Lewkowicz, & T. Bokanowski (Eds.), *On Freud's "Mourning and Melancholia* (pp. 90–109). London: Karnac.

Walter, T. (2014). Organizations and death–a view from death studies. *Culture and Organization, 20*(1): 68–76.

Weatherill, R. (1999). The death drive: new life for a dead subject. *Encyclopaedia of Psychoanalysis, 3*: 1–11.

Whetten, D. A. (1980). Organizational decline: a neglected topic in organizational science. *Academy of Management Review, 5*(4): 577–588.

Whetten, D. A. (1987). Organizational growth and decline processes. *Annual Review of Sociology, 13*(1): 335–358.

Winnicott, D. W. (1975). *Through Pediatrics to Psychoanalysis: The Collected Papers of D. W. Winnicott*. New York: Basic Books.

Zell, D. (2003). Organizational change as a process of death, dying, and rebirth. *Journal of Applied Behavioural Science, 39*(1): 73–96.

INDEX

173